5 STEP ENGLISH

The Old Man and the Sea
LEVEL 1~3

5단계로 술술 읽히는 영어원서
단계영어 노인과 바다 LEVEL 1~3

초판 | 1쇄 인쇄 2022년 1월 17일
개정 | 1쇄 발행 2025년 4월 10일

지 은 이 | 어니스트 헤밍웨이
영어번역 | Steve Oh, HannahAllyse Kim
정보맵핑 | 이야기 연구소
그　 　림 | 김영미
감　 　수 | Jinny Lee / HannahAllyse Kim / Edmund Nai /
제 작 처 | 다온피앤피
특허등록 | 10-2020-0012558
국제출원 | PCT/KR2020/002551

펴 낸 곳 | (주)도서출판동행
펴 낸 이 | 오승근
출판등록 | 2020년 3월 20일 제2020-000005호
주　 　소 | 부산광역시 부산진구 동천로109, 9층
이 메 일 | withyou@withyoubooks.com
카카오톡 | @도서출판동행

단계별 요약정보 기술은 국내특허등록 및 PCT 국제출원을 했습니다.

이 책은 저작권법에 따라 보호받는 저작물이므로 무단 전재와 복제를 금지하며, 이 책 내용의 전부 또는 일부를 이용하려면 반드시 출판사의 서면 동의를 받아야 합니다.
잘못된 책은 구입하신 서점에서 바꿔 드립니다.

ISBN 979-11-91648-35-5

단계영어

노인과 바다

LEVEL 1~3

Prologue 머리말

　인터넷에서 사용되는 언어의 55.7%가 영어입니다. 인터넷 정보의 절반 이상이 영어로 존재하는 현실 속에서, 영어를 잘 모른다는 것은 그만큼 많은 정보로부터 단절된다는 의미이기도 합니다. 그렇다면 한국어는 인터넷에서 어느 정도 비중을 차지할까요? 놀랍게도 한국어는 인터넷 전체 언어의 1%도 채 되지 않는 0.4%에 불과합니다.

　물론 영어를 안다고 해서 인터넷상의 모든 영어 정보를 완벽히 이해할 수 있는 건 아닙니다. 하지만 할 수 있는데 하지 않는 것과 처음부터 할 수 없는 것에는 분명한 차이가 있습니다.

　영어의 "말하기, 듣기, 읽기, 쓰기" 중 중요하지 않은 영역은 없습니다. 그중에서도 인터넷을 삶의 일부로 살아가는 우리에게 가장 필요한 영역은 단연 '읽기'일 것입니다. 영어 읽기는 책을 읽듯 자연스럽게 이루어지는 것이 중요합니다. 하지만 현실은 그렇지 않습니다. 어렵고 긴 문장, 낯선 어휘 때문에 페이지를 넘기기조차 쉽지 않다는 것을 경험해 보셨을 겁니다. 사전을 일일이 찾지 않고 문맥에서 유추하는 것은 좋지만, 모르는 단어가 매 문장마다 등장한다면 어떻게 내용을 이해할 수 있을까요?

　바로 여기에 『단계영어』의 진정한 가치가 있습니다. 『단계영어』는 마치 어린아이가 모국어를 배우듯, 쉬운 단계에서 점차 어려운 단계로 나아가며 자연스럽게 영어를 익힐 수 있도록 구성된 책입니다. 아이들이 처음 말을 배울 때를 떠올려

보세요. 처음에는 단지 "엄마, 밥 줘"라고 짧고 간단한 문장만 구사하다가도 시간이 지나면서 "엄마, 내가 좋아하는 김밥 먹고 싶어요."처럼 더 길고 구체적인 표현을 하게 됩니다. 하지만 중요한 점은 표현 방식이 바뀌었을 뿐, 전달하고자 하는 핵심은 동일하다는 것입니다.다. 그러니까 처음엔 "엄마 밥 줘"였는데, 시간이 지나면 "엄마 내가 좋아하는 김밥 먹고 싶어요" 처럼 표현에 깊이가 생긴다는 것이죠.

『단계영어』의 구성 또한 이와 같습니다. 레벨1부터 레벨5까지의 과정은 아이가 몇 년 동안 언어를 습득하며 성장하는 과정을 담고 있습니다. 레벨1은 가장 쉬운 어휘와 짧은 문장으로, 레벨2는 조금 더 다양한 어휘와 복잡한 표현으로 구성되어 있습니다. 레벨1을 읽고 이해할 수 있다면, 레벨2는 사전 없이도 충분히 내용을 유추하며 읽어낼 수 있을 것입니다. 믿기 어렵다고요? 이미 수많은 독자들의 생생한 후기가 이를 증명하고 있습니다.

다시 한번 강조하지만, 책은 '읽어야' 합니다. 편안한 마음으로 부담 없이 읽으세요. 정확한 해석이나 완벽한 이해를 목표로 하지 않아도 괜찮습니다. 틀려도 좋습니다. 생각해 보세요. 성인인 우리도 모국어를 자주 틀리지 않습니까? 틀림을 두려워하지 말고, 그냥 편안하게 읽어 보세요.

사실 아이들이 언어를 배우는 과정 또한 수많은 실수의 연속입니다. 발음도 어순도 잘못된 단어도 계속 틀립니다. 하지만 지속적으로 언어를 사용하면서 틀린 부분을 스스로 고쳐가며 결국 완벽한 언어 능력을 갖추게 됩니다. 언어 습득에 가장 중요한 것은 바로 '지속성'입니다.

『단계영어』는 특별한 준비 없이도 언제든 펼쳐볼 수 있게 구성되어, 영어 읽기의 지속성을 유지하기에 최적의 도구가 될 것입니다. 지금 바로 레벨1을 펼쳐보세요. 머지않아 여러분은 다음 레벨이 기다려질 만큼 영어 읽기가 즐거워질 것입니다.

자, 이제 『단계영어』와 함께 영어 읽기의 새로운 여정을 시작해 보세요!

Steve,Oh

"고졸 학력 30대 직장인입니다. 학생 때도 영어와는 담쌓고 살았습니다. 영어를 무기로 좋은 기회 잡는 사람들을 볼 때마다 한번은 영어를 정복하겠다고 막연히 생각했습니다. "영어 일기, 원서 읽기, 쉐도우 리딩, 토익 문제 풀이" 등 시중에 많은 영어 학습법이 있었지만, 기초가 없다 보니 힘들더군요. 사전 찾느라 한 시간에 한 페이지 겨우 할까 말까 하다 보니 금방 그만두게 됐습니다. 뜻을 유추하는 것도 앞뒤는 알고 하나만 모를 때 통하지 아예 모르면 안 되더라고요. 그러다 와디즈 통해서 『단계영어』 시리즈를 알게 되어 지금은 레벨1을 지나 레벨2 초입을 읽고 있습니다. 레벨1은 일단 쉬웠습니다. 모르거나 모호하게 아는 단어가 없진 않았지만, 레벨1에서는 유추할 수 있었습니다. 진도가 잘 나가다 보니 재미 붙여서 꾸준히 읽혔습니다. 레벨2로 넘어와도 아는 내용, 아는 문장이라 그런지 술술 넘어갑니다. 이런 식으로 책 한 권 읽고 추가로 나올 단계 영어 두 세 권 더 읽고 나면 독해는 충분하겠다는 자신감이 생깁니다."

- 포천 흥님

"초보자가 쉽게 접근할 수 있는 책 구성이 좋았습니다. 중간마다 들어 있는 삽화도 마음에 들었어요. 쉬는 시간마다 잠깐씩 읽고 있는데 제가 아직 꾸준히 읽고 있다는 게 놀랍네요. 매번 영어 원서를 사놓고 전시만 하던 제가 이런 끈기가 있다는 것을 알게 해주셔서 고맙습니다.

저는 첫 단계를 읽을 때 모르는 단어를 사전 찾지 않고 먼저 노트에 정리만 했어요. 그리고 첫 단계를 다 읽은 뒤에 노트에 적은 단어를 찾아가며 다시 읽었습니다. 이렇게 읽으니 그다음 단계를 읽고 싶은 도전이 생겨서 좋았습니다."

- 상도동 필릭스님

"처음으로 산 『단계영어』 시리즈입니다. <노인과 바다>처럼 권위 있는 문학상을 받은 작품이라고 하면 대체로 일반인들이 읽기가 어렵습니다. 그런데 한글로도 읽기 어려운 작품을 영어로 읽는다니 다른 세상 이야기라 생각했습니다. 하지만 단계별 영어원서 구성이 제 마음을 붙잡았습니다. 쉬운 영어로 전체 내용을 알려주고 점차 어려운 표현으로 레벨을 올리며 반복해 결국 원문을 어렵지 않게 읽을 수 있게 해 준다는 개념에 책을 구매하게 됐습니다.

우선 책 곳곳에 있는 삽화들이 좋았습니다. 특히 물고기 종류나 낚시 도구 같은 모르는 단어를 그림을 통해 알 수 있게 해줘서 글을 이해하는 데 도움이 되었고, 그림이 글 중간마다 있는 것 자체가 지루함을 줄여 주었습니다. 레벨1부터 욕심내지 않고 하루에 한 챕터씩 보고 있습니다. 모르는 단어도 있지만, 그냥 한글 소설 보듯이 추측하며 넘어가고 있습니다. 레벨의 효과가 궁금해 챕터 1에 대한 레벨별 비교를 해 봤습니다. 레벨1에서 3까지는 괜찮았는데 레벨4부터는 모르는 단어가 급격히 늘어나더군요. 하지만 내용을 이미 알고 있어 읽는 데 큰 어려움이 없었습니다. 단계별 읽기의 힘이라고 생각합니다.

『단계영어』 노인과 바다 편은 사전 없이 높은 수준의 책을 원서로 읽을 수 있는 즐거움과 성취감을 주는 좋은 책이라 생각합니다. 특히나 문학작품은 번역으로는 전달하기 힘든 그 언어의 고유한 감성이 있다고들 합니다. 그런 점에서 『단계영어』의 시도는 원작자의 의도를 더 가깝게 이해할 소중한 기회의 시작이 될 수 있다고 생각합니다. 앞으로 좋은 작품으로 다시 만날 수 있기를 기대합니다."

- 수내동 와디즈잇님

"아이들 졸업 선물로 준비했는데, 아이들 모두 무척 좋아했어요! 소장용 하나, 학습용 하나 두고 천천히 보고 있어요! 레벨별로 쓰인 어휘가 다르다 보니, 어휘량도 늘고 리딩 훈련에 도움이 됩니다!"

- 익명의서포터님

Manual 사용설명서

한 번 상상해 보세요.
세계문학을 원서로 읽는다면, 얼마나 유익할까요?

독서가 중요한 것은 누구나 아는 사실입니다. 그 중요한 독서를 영어로 할 수 있다면 얼마나 좋을까요? 한 번 상상해보세요. 세계문학을 원서로 읽고 있는 자신의 모습을 말이에요. 한 마디로 '독서'와 '영어 공부', 이 두 마리 토끼를 다 잡은 것입니다. 그런데 문제는 이게 말처럼 쉽지 않다는 것이죠.

대부분 영어 원서는 책처럼 쭉 읽기가 어렵습니다. 어려운 단어들과 긴 문장 때문입니다. 그런데 어려운 단어로 표현하려는 내용은 쉬운 단어로 바꿔 표현이 가능합니다. 긴 문장 역시 짧은 문장 2~3개로 나눌 수 있습니다. 쉬운 단어와 짧은 문장으로 책 전체 내용을 먼저 읽은 뒤, 단어의 난도를 단계적으로 높이고 문장의 길이 또한 단계적으로 늘린다면 누구나 쉽게 원서를 읽을 수 있지 않을까요?

『단계영어 노인과 바다』는 이러한 방식을 통해 '독서와 영어 공부'라는 두 마리 토끼를 잡게 해드립니다. 방법도 어렵지 않습니다. 다음에 나오는 4가지 방법을 따라 그냥 책 읽듯이 책장을 넘기시면 됩니다.

단계별 영어 도서
오디오북 채널

1 영어 공부가 아닌 책을 읽는다고 생각하세요.

   이게 가장 중요한 부분입니다. 우리가 어떻게 책을 읽는지 생각해보세요. 우리는 일반적으로 책을 읽을 때 국어사전을 찾아가며 읽지 않습니다. 책을 계속 읽다 보면 아까 그 단어가 이런 뜻이구나 하며 자연스럽게 넘어갑니다. 이렇게 책을 읽는다는 생각으로 단계 영어를 읽어보세요.

2 레벨 1부터 읽으세요.

   레벨1이 쉽게 보여도 일단 레벨 1부터 읽어야 다음 단계로 수월하게 올라갈 수 있습니다. 마치 계단을 오를 때, 첫 번째 계단에 발을 내딛고 그다음 계단으로 올라가는 것처럼 말입니다. 게다가 레벨 1은 책을 이해하는 데 가장 중요한 뼈대가 됩니다.

3 모르는 단어가 나와도 사전을 먼저 찾지 마세요.

   사전은 책을 다 읽었는데도 그 단어 때문에 책 내용이 이해가 안 되거나, 그 단어의 뜻을 정확히 알고 싶어질 때 찾으시면 됩니다.

4 레벨 5까지 읽으셨다면 이제 레벨 4, 3, 2, 1 순으로 읽어보세요.

   복잡한 문장들이 어떻게 간략하게 요약되는지, 내 영어 실력이 어느 정도 성장했는지를 파악할 수 있습니다.

『단계영어』 노인과 바다는
쉬운 핵심문장부터 단계적으로 읽어
영어를 쉽게 이해할 수 있습니다.

책의 특징

01 높은 곳을 계단으로 한 걸음씩 오르는 것처럼, 어려운 영어 원문을 레벨에 따라 한 단계씩 읽을 수 있게 만든 책입니다. 레벨에 따라 차례대로 읽으면, 노인과 바다 영어 원문도 사전 없이 자연스럽게 읽게 됩니다.

02 레벨 1부터 레벨 4까지의 노인과 바다 본문은 레벨 5인 원문을 자연스럽게 읽을 수 있도록 단계별 정보설계 기술로 제작되었습니다.

03 원문의 중요한 부분만 발췌 편집한 것이 아닌 원문을 논리적 단계로 요약해서 만들었기에, 레벨별 문단 수와 챕터 수가 원문과 거의 동일합니다.

셀프 테스트

레벨 1을 몇 장 읽어보시고, '이 정도면 읽을 수 있겠다.'라는 생각이 든다면 이 책을 시작하셔도 괜찮습니다. 만약 레벨 1이 어렵다면, 조금 더 쉬운 "어린 왕자", "행복한 왕자, "잠자는 숲 속의 공주"를 추천해 드립니다.

단계별 특징

LEVEL 1

구 성 원문의 핵심을 가장 쉬운 단어와 문장으로 재구성했습니다.

효 과 영어 자신감 향상!
원문 정보를 표현할 수 있는 쉬운(필수) 단어와 문장이 당신의 영어 자신감을 한 층 성장시킬 것입니다.

빠른 도서 내용 파악
원문 핵심이 들어 있어 전체 내용을 빠르게 이해할 수 있습니다.

성취감 형성
레벨 1은 짧고 쉽지만, 독립된 한 권의 책입니다.
레벨 1을 다 읽었다면 노인과 바다 영어 원서를 일독한 것입니다.

LEVEL 2

구 성 레벨 1의 문장 구조에 기본 서술 문장이 추가되었습니다.

효 과 독서 속도 향상!
이미 읽은 핵심 문장 구조가 있기에 레벨 1보다 빠른 속도로 읽기가 가능합니다.

Manual 사용설명서

LEVEL 3

구 성   핵심 정보에 추가되는 내용과 레벨 2보다 한 단계 높은 단어와 문장으로 되어 있습니다.

효 과   자연스러운 단어 유추
레벨 1, 2를 통해 기본 단어와 문장 구조가 파악되어 한 단계 높아진 단어와 추가된 문장들도 유추하며 읽을 수 있습니다.

LEVEL 4

구 성   레벨 5인 원문을 자연스럽게 읽을 수 있게 만들어 놓은 단계입니다.

자 기 신 뢰   이미 노인과 바다를 세 번 읽은 당신에게 레벨 4는 어렵지 않게 읽을 수 있는 단계가 되었습니다.

효 과   독해 능력 향상
레벨 5 원문을 자연스럽게 읽을 수 있게 도와줍니다.

LEVEL 5

드디어 원문입니다. 난생처음 보는 단어들과 관용어들을 만나게 됩니다. 하지만 두려울 필요가 없습니다. 당신에게는 레벨 4가 있습니다. 막히는 단어는 사전을 찾기 전 레벨4를 통해 유추해 보세요. 이렇게 상상하며 단어 뜻을 찾았을 때 그 단어는 오랫동안 당신의 기억 속에 자리 잡게 됩니다.

● Words 이미지 단어

sardine

skiff

gaff

harpoon

flying fish

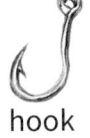
hook

albacore

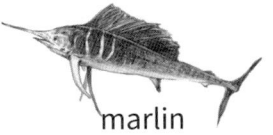
marlin

dolphin(만새기)

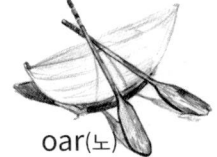
oar(노)

● Words 이미지 단어

man-of-war bird

Portuguese man-of-war

porpoise

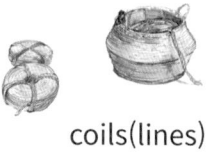
coils(lines)

sack

loggerheads

hawk-bill

green turtle

● Words 이미지 단어

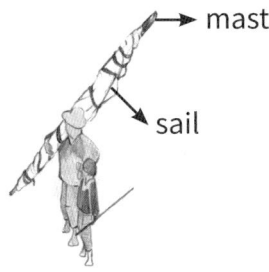
mast
sail

royal palm

mako shark

warbler

shovel-nosed shark

dark tern

cast net

<fishing hook>

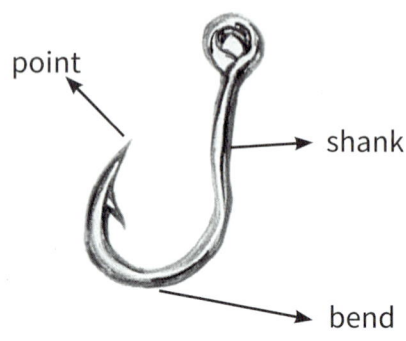

<skiff>

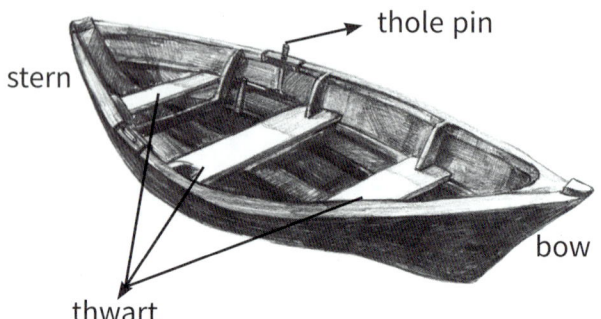

Contentrds 차례

단계별 영어 도서
오디오북 채널

머리말	4
독자후기	6
사용설명서	8
이미지단어	13

The Old Man and the Sea **LEVEL 1**

CHAPTER 1~4	**21~24**
CHAPTER 5~8	**29~35**
CHAPTER 9~12	**37~43**
CHAPTER 13~16	**45~52**
CHAPTER 17~20	**54~60**
CHAPTER 21~24	**63~71**
CHAPTER 25~28	**72~79**

The Old Man and the Sea **LEVEL 2**

CHAPTER 1~3	**83~88**
CHAPTER 4~6	**91~97**
CHAPTER 7~9	**99~104**
CHAPTER 10~12	**108~112**

The Old Man and the Sea LEVEL 2

CHAPTER 13~15	114~118
CHAPTER 16~18	121~126
CHAPTER 19~21	128~134
CHAPTER 22~24	137~143
CHAPTER 25~28	144~152

The Old Man and the Sea LEVEL 3

CHAPTER 1~2	157~159
CHAPTER 3~4	162~166
CHAPTER 5~6	170~173
CHAPTER 7~8	176~180
CHAPTER 9~10	182~186
CHAPTER 11~12	190~193
CHAPTER 13~14	195~198
CHAPTER 15~16	201~204
CHAPTER 17~18	207~211
CHAPTER 19~20	214~218
CHAPTER 21~22	221~225
CHAPTER 23~24	229~234
CHAPTER 25~26	236~241
CHAPTER 27~28	243~247

노인과 바다 핵심을 쉬운 단어와 짧은 문장으로 재구성 했습니다.

잃어버린 영어 자존심을 Level 1 단계에서 찾으세요.

THE ORIGINAL TEXT

"Be patient, hand," he said. "I do this for you." I wish I could feed the fish, he thought. He is my brother. But I must kill him and keep strong to do it. Slowly and conscientiously he ate all of the wedge-shaped strips of fish. He straightened up, wiping his hand on his trousers.

LEVEL 1

**"Hold on, hand," he said.
"I do this for you."
He ate all of the fish.**

The Old Man and the Sea

LEVEL 1

Chapter 1
The Old Man and the Boy

He was an old fisherman. He caught nothing for 84 days. The boy who was with him went to another boat.

The old man's empty boat made the boy sad. The boy always went down to help him carry his fishing stuff.

The old man was thin. He had deep wrinkles. Brown age spots were on his cheeks, and his hands had deep old scars.

He was old, but his eyes were bright.
"**Santiago**, I could go with you again," the boy said.
"No. You're with a lucky boat. Stay with them," the old man said.

"But remember last time. We caught some big fish."

"I remember," the old man said. "But you have to obey your Papa."

"Yes," the boy said. "Can I buy a beer for you on the Terrace?"

"Why not?" the old man said.

They sat on the Terrace. Other fishermen were there.

Chapter 2
Friendship

The successful fishermen carried their fish to the fish house. The fish would go to the market in Havana.

The other fishermen caught sharks. They moved the

sharks to the shark factory.

The wind blew in from the north. There was no bad smell from the shark factory. The Terrace was pleasant and sunny.

"**Santiago**! Can I go out to get some small fish for you?" the boy said.
"No, Thank you."
"I would like to help you in some way."
"You bought me a beer," the old man said.

"How old was I when you first took me in a boat?"
"You were five years old. We caught a tough fish. Do you remember?"
"I remember the fishtail hitting the boat. You were hitting the fish."

"Can you really remember that?"
"I remember everything."
"If you were my boy, we would go fishing together..."
"May I get some small fish?"
"I have mine here."
"Let me get four fish."
"Just one is okay," the old man said.
"Two," the boy said.
"Two," the old man agreed.

"Tomorrow will be a good day to catch fish," the old man said.

"Where are you going?" the boy asked.
"I will go far out."

"I'll ask him to go far and catch fish," the boy said. "If you catch big fish, we can help you."
"He does not like to fish too far out."
"But he can't see far. So I'll tell him there are fish far out," the boy said.

"Are his eyes that bad?"
"He is almost blind."
"It is strange," the old man said. "He never went to catch sea turtles. Looking for sea turtles kills the eyes."
"But you went to catch sea turtles, and your eyes are good."
"I am a strange old man."
"But are you strong? Can you catch a big fish?"
"I think so."

"Let us take the stuff home," the boy said.

They picked up the stuff from the boat. The stuff was the mast, wooden box, gaff, and harpoon. It was not a good idea to leave the stuff on the boat.

Chapter 3
The Shack

They walked together into the old man's small house. They put the stuff down.

The small house was made of palm trees. There was a

bed, a table, and one chair in the house. There were two pictures on the wall. The old man's clean shirt was on the shelf.

"Do you have something to eat?" the boy asked.
"A pot of yellow rice with fish. Do you want some?"
"No, I will eat at home. Do you want me to make the fire?"

"No. I will make it later on."
There was no pot of yellow rice and fish but they made up this story every day.
"85 is a lucky number," the old man said.
"I'll catch some small fish. Will you sit in the doorway?"
"Yes, I will read the newspaper."
The old man took the newspaper out from under the

bed.

"**Perico** gave this newspaper to me," he said.

"I'll be back when I have some small fish. When I come back, you can tell me about the baseball game."

"The **New York Yankees** will win."

"But I am worried about the **Cleveland Indians**."

"Have faith in the **New York Yankees**."

"When I come back, tell me more."

"Should we buy a lottery ticket? How about a ticket with the number 85?" the old man said. "Tomorrow is the 85th day."

"Sure. I can order one. Keep warm, old man," the boy said. " I will go now to get the small fish."

The boy came back. The old man was sleeping in the chair. The boy covered the old man with a blanket. The old man looked strong, but he was old. He was wearing an old shirt. He didn't have shoes.

Chapter 4
The Baseball Game

The boy left him there. When he came back, the old man was still sleeping.

"Wake up old man," the boy said.
"What did you bring?" the old man asked.
"I brought some food."
"I'm not very hungry."
"You can't go fishing if you don't eat."
The old man got up and said, "What are we eating?"
"Black beans and rice," the boy answered.
"Who gave this to you?"
"**Martin**. The owner of the Terrace."
"I need to thank him."
"I thanked him already," the boy said.
"I will give him some fish."

"Should we eat?" the old man said, "your food is good."
"Tell me about the baseball game," the boy asked him.
"The best team is the **Yankees**," the old man said happily.
"But today, they lost the game," the boy told him.
"It is okay. The great **DiMaggio** is doing well again."
"What about the other baseball team?" the boy asked.
"There is the **Philadelphia** team. **Dick Sisler** is there."
"Do you remember **Dick Sisler** came here?" the old man said.
"I wanted to go fishing with him. But I was too shy to ask him. It was a great mistake," the boy said. "Tell me about the great **John J. McGraw**."
"He came to the Terrace sometimes. He loved horse racing as well as baseball."
"He was a great manager," the boy said. "My father thinks he was the greatest."

"That's because your father saw him many times," the old man said.

"Who is the greatest manager, **Luque** or **Mike Gonzalez**?" the boy asked.
"I think they are the same."
"And the best fisherman is you."
"There are many people who are better than me."
"No, you are the best."
"Thank you. You make me happy. You have to sleep now."
"Good night! You're my alarm clock," the boy said.
"I'll wake you up in time."
"Good night, old man."
"Good night, boy."

Chapter 5
Going Fishing

The boy went out. They ate in the dark. The old man went to bed.

He went to sleep fast. He dreamed of Africa. He saw the beaches in his dream. He saw the big brown mountains too. He smelled the smell of Africa.

When he smelled the smell of Africa, he woke up. But

tonight, he smelled it earlier. He dreamed a long dream. He saw the white mountain of the Islands.

He only dreamed of places and lions on the beach. He loved lions, and he loved the boy. The old man woke up. He went to wake up the boy. The outside air was cold.

He went to the boy's house. The boy was sleeping in the first room. The old man woke the boy up. The boy woke up and looked at him. The old man went out and the boy went out too.

The old man said, "I am sorry."

"No, it is what I have to do," the boy said.

They went to the old man's small house. They took the fishing stuff with them.

"Do you want coffee?" the boy asked.

"Let's put the stuff in the boat first," the old man answered. They had coffee together.

"How did you sleep?" the boy asked.
"Very good, Manolin," the old man said.
"So did I," the boy said. "I'll get some small fish for you."
"Thank you," the old man said.
"I'll be right back," the boy said.

He went to the ice house. The old man drank his coffee. For a long time, he didn't carry a lunch box with him. He had only a bottle of water.

The boy came back. They went down to the boat.
"Good luck, old man."
"Good luck," the old man said.
He began to row. There were other boats going out to sea.

Chapter 6
Bait

The boats were quiet. They moved further out. They wanted to find fish. The old man rowed. He wanted to go far.

He rowed over to one place. The fishermen called this

place "the great well." There were many fish there.

The old man could feel the morning coming. He heard the flying fish. The flying fish were his good friends.

The old man was sorry for the small birds. He thought that the birds had a hard time. Why were the small birds weak?

The old man thought the sea was kind. People thought of the sea as a woman. The younger fishermen thought of the sea as a man. The old man always thought of the sea as a woman.

He was rowing along. The sea was peaceful. It was daylight now. He didn't know he was further out. Then he saw where he was.
He thought, "Today I will go where many fish go."

He threw his baits out before it was light. Four baits were down in the water. They were in different deep places. The bait fish were tied to the hooks. The hooks had many sweet-smelling fish.
The boy gave him two small fish. The small fish hung on the two deepest fishing lines. The lines were thick. They were like a pencil. Each line was very long.

Now the old man rowed softly. Light was coming. The old man could see the other boats. Then the sun was very bright. The bright light hurt his eyes. He rowed his boat. He did not look at the sun.

He watched the fishing lines. The lines went straight down into the water. He kept the lines in the right place.

He thought, "I have no luck. But who knows? Maybe today is the day."

Chapter 7
A Man-Of-War Bird

The sun had come up. It was high in the sky. There were only three boats in sight.

He thought, "My eyes hurt in the morning sun. But my eyes are okay in the evening sun."

Just then, he saw a big bird. The bird was flying in a circle.

"The bird's got something," the old man said.

He rowed toward the bird.

The bird flew higher. Then the bird came down very fast.

"Big dolphin," the old man said.

He brought a small fishing line. He threw the line over the side of the boat. He was rowing again. He was watching the big bird.

The old man saw the flying fish. The bird tried to catch the flying fish. The dolphin followed the flying fish.

The old man watched the flying fish and the bird.

He thought, "The fish are moving too fast. It is hard to catch them."

Far away, the land was like a green line. The water was so dark. There were the plankton in the dark water. He was happy to see the plankton.

The sun came up higher. The weather was good. But there was nothing around. There was no bird around. There were no fish around. There was only one big jellyfish. The jellyfish had poison inside.

"This is bad water," the old man said.

He looked into the water. There were tiny fish. They were strong. The jellyfish poison did not hurt the fish. But humans

were not strong. Sometimes the jellyfish hurt the old man.

The jellyfish were beautiful. But they were dangerous. The old man loved sea turtles. The turtles ate the jellyfish.

He loved **green** turtles and **hawk-bill** turtles. He didn't like **loggerhead** turtles.

He had hunted turtles. He was sorry for them all. Most people do not think about turtles.

But the old man thought, "The turtles and I are no different."

Chapter 8
Albacore

The old man looked up. The bird was flying in a circle again. A small tuna jumped out of the water. Then the tuna jumped all around.

He watched the group of tuna and the bird.

"The bird is a great help," the old man said.

A small tuna got caught on the fishing line. The old man pulled the tuna in. The tuna's tail moved fast in the boat. The old man hit the tuna.

"This is **Albacore**," he said. "It will be good for bait."
He talked to himself.

He talked to himself after the boy left. The old man and the boy did not talk very much.

"If others heard me talking, they would think I am crazy," he said. "But I am not crazy."

"I will focus on fishing. Maybe a big fish is here," he thought.

The old man could not see the land. He could see the clouds. The clouds looked like high mountains. The sea was very dark. The old man saw the deep blue sea. He saw his fishing lines.

Chapter 9
Encounter

The tunas were gone. The sun was hot. The old man felt it on the back of his neck.

"I could fall asleep," the old man thought.

Just then, the fishing line went down.
"Yes," he said. "Yes."
He held the fishing line. He felt a fish pulling the fishing line.

The old man untied the line.
"This fish must be huge," he thought. "Eat the baits, fish. Eat them. Please eat them."
He felt a slight pull. Then there was nothing.

"Come on," the old man shouted. "Turn! Come back! Just smell them. Don't be shy, fish. Eat them."
He waited. He held the fishing line. He felt a pull on the line.

"The fish will eat the bait," the old man said.
But the old man felt nothing.
"The fish did not go," he said. "The fish is coming."
Then he felt the fishing line.
"The fish moved," he said. "He will eat it."

He was happy. He felt the fishing line. He felt something strong. He felt something heavy. It was the big fish. He let the line go down. He felt the big fish.

"What a fish," he said.
"The fish will eat the bait," the old man thought.
He knew the fish was big. The fish did not move. The fish was heavy. The fishing line went down.

"The fish bit the bait," he said. "I will let the fish eat."
He prepared more fishing lines.

"Eat more," he said.
"Okay. Are you ready?" he thought.
"Now!" he shouted.
He pulled up the fishing line.

Nothing happened. The old man could not pull the fish in. He held the line. The boat moved ahead.

The fish moved. The baits were in the water.

"I miss the boy," the old man said. "The fish is pulling the boat. I have to hold this fishing line. The fish is not going down."

He held the fishing line. The boat was moving.
"The fish will stop soon," the old man thought.
But the fish kept swimming. The fish was pulling the boat.

"I caught the fish at noon," the old man said. "I have not seen it."
His hat hurt his head. He was thirsty too. He opened his water bottle. He drank water.

He looked back. He could not see the land.
"The fish will come up soon," he thought. "The fish has the hook in its mouth. The fish is hurting."

Chapter 10
Moving Along

The old man looked at the sky. There were stars. The sun went down. It was cold. The old man put a sack on his back. The sack was like a cushion.

"There's nothing I can do with the fish," he thought.

The old man looked at the stars. He checked his course. The boat was moving. The boat was slow. The light of the land was not strong. The boat was going east.

He remembered the baseball game. But he focused on fishing.

"I wish the boy were here," he said.
"I must remember to eat the tuna tomorrow. I need to keep strong," he said to himself.

Two dolphins followed the boat.
"They are good. They are friends of mine," he said.

He thought of the big fish. He felt sad.
"How old is this fish? This fish is calm. This is very strange," he thought. "The fish doesn't know I'm alone. The fish is brave. What a great fish."

The old man remembered a story. This happened in the past. He caught a marlin fish.

There were two marlins. One was a male. One was a female. The old man caught the female fish. The male fish stayed with the female fish. The old man hit the female fish. The old man put the female fish on the boat. The male fish was still by the boat. The old man prepared the spear. The male fish jumped. Then the male fish went away.

"The male fish was wonderful," the old man remembered.

"I wish the boy were here," he said.
He leaned against the front of the boat.

"We are all alone," the old man thought. "You were hiding. I found you. I'm a true fisherman."

Chapter 11
Tug-of-war

Something took the bait. The fishing line went into the water. The old man had a knife. He cut two fishing lines. He tied the fishing lines. He had six more fishing lines.

"I will cut some of the line and tie it up," he thought. "I lost a good fishing line. I can buy a fishing line again. But I did not lose that big fish. I could not catch that big fish again. What was it? Was it a marlin? Was it a shark?"

"I wish the boy were here," he said.
"But the boy is not here. Only you are here," he thought.
The old man worked in the boat with the fishing lines. The big fish moved. The old man fell down. The old man rested in the boat.

The old man moved the fishing line. He felt the fish move. He felt the speed of the boat.

"Why did the fish move?" he thought. "Maybe the fish got hurt. But I have pain in my back. The fish will be tired. The fish can't swim forever."

"Fish," he said softly. "I'll stay with you."
"The fish will stay with me too," the old man thought.
It was cold. He waited for the sun.
"The fish can do it, so I can do it," he thought.

The boat moved. The sun came up. The old man held the fishing line. The line was on his shoulder.

"He's going north," the old man said.
"I wish the fish was tired," he thought.
The sun went up. The fish was swimming up.

"God, help the fish jump," the old man said. "I have enough fishing line. I can get the fish."

He pulled on the fishing line. But the line didn't move.
"I will not pull more," he thought. "The hook might fall out. Anyway, I feel good. Now I am not looking at the sun."

There was a yellow sea plant on the fishing line. The yellow sea plant made light.
"Fish," he said.
"I love you, but I will kill you," he thought.

Chapter 12
A Small Bird

A small bird came to the boat. The small bird was tired. The bird sat on the boat. The bird flew to the fishing line.

"How old are you?" the old man asked the bird. "Is this your first trip?"

"This fishing line is steady," the old man said to the bird. "What happened? Why are you so tired?"

"Take a good rest, small bird," he said. "You can stay at my house. I can't take you back. I'm sorry. I am with a big fish."

Then the fish moved fast. The old man fell down. The bird flew away.

His right hand was bleeding.
"Something hurt the fish," he said.
He pulled on the fishing line.

"You're feeling it now," the old man said to the fish.
He looked for the bird. The bird was gone.
"Why did I fall?" he thought. "I was looking at the small bird. I will think about work now."
"I miss the boy," he said.

Chapter 13
Left Hand

The old man washed his hand in the sea. The blood washed away.

"Now, the fish is slow," he said.
The old man's hand was in the water. The old man stood up. The old man lifted his hand. The cut was not deep. The old man was mad. He needed his hand for work.

"I will eat the tuna," he said.
He found the tuna. He cut the tuna into pieces.
"I don't think I can eat all of this," he said.
His left hand could not move. His left hand had a cramp.

"What is wrong? My hand has a cramp," he said.
"Eat the tuna now," he thought.
He ate some tuna.
"The fish tastes good," he thought. "I want to eat it with salt."
"How do you feel, hand?" the old man asked his hand.
He had a cramp. His hand was stiff.
"I'll eat more for you." He ate more fish.
"How are you, hand?" said the old man. He ate more fish.

"The tuna is a healthy fish," he thought. "I am happy. I have this tuna. I'm not hungry. But I need to eat."

"Hold on, hand," he said. "I do this for you." He ate all of the fish.

"Hand, you can let the fishing line go," he said. "I will hold the line with my right arm."

"God, heal my hand," he said. "I don't know what the fish is going to do."

"What is the fish's plan?" he thought. "If the fish stays down, I will stay down."

He tried to open his hand. His hand would not open.

"Maybe my hand will open in the daytime," he thought. "I will let my hand open little by little. I have used this hand too much."

Chapter 14
Jumping Up

The old man felt alone. But he could see beautiful things in the water. The clouds were big in the sky. He saw wild ducks flying together. Only this man was on the sea. No other man was alone on the sea.

Some people are scared of the sea. Sometimes the

weather is bad. But there are no big storms. The weather is good.

You can see big storms on the sea. But the land is far away. It is hard to see the storms.

He looked at the sky.
"The breeze is good," he said. "This is a good day."

His left hand was getting better.
"I do not like cramps," he thought. "My body is having trouble."

"If the boy were here, he would help me," he thought.

Then, he felt something. It was the fishing line. The fishing line was coming up.
"The fish is coming up!" he said.
The fishing line came up. The fish came out. The fish was bright. The fish was dark purple. His sword was long. The fish went into the water.

"The fish is longer than the boat," the old man said.
The fishing line went down. The old man held the fishing line.

"I need to catch the fish," he thought. "The fish is strong. But the fish does not know. I am glad. The fish does not know that."

The old man met many big fish. But this was his first time alone with a big fish. His left hand felt bad.

"My hand will be okay," he thought. "My left hand will help my right hand. They are brothers."
The fish moved slowly.

"Why did the fish jump?" the old man thought. "Now I know. The fish is so big. I can show the fish who I am."

Chapter 15
The Prayer

The old man rested. The boat moved. There was a small wave on the sea. It was noon. The old man's hand felt good.

"Bad news for you, fish," he said.
"I don't have faith," he said.
"But I will pray ten times."

He began to pray. He was so tired, but he kept praying.

He felt good, but he also felt pain. He rested in the boat.

The sun was hot. The wind was soft.

"I have no more food. I'll catch another fish. I want to catch a flying fish. Flying fish taste good," he said.
"This fish is so big," he thought.
"I will kill the fish," he said.

The old man caught big fish in the past. But he wanted to do it again.
"I have to catch the fish now. I will prove that I'm still lucky," he said.

"I want the fish to fall asleep. I want to sleep too. I want to dream about lions. But why do I see lions in my dreams?" he thought.
"Do not think, old man," he said to himself. "Take a rest."

The boat still moved slowly. The wind blew from the east. The fish slowed down.

The fishing line came up in the afternoon. The sun was on the old man's left arm.

The old man saw the fish once. He thought of the fish swimming. "Big eyes help the fish to see. The fish has huge eyes. How well can the fish see in the dark?" he thought.
His left hand felt good. The left hand helped the right hand.
"If you are not tired, fish," he said. "You are strange."

The old man was very tired. He tried to think of other things. He thought of baseball games.

"Who won the baseball game?" he thought. "The great **DiMaggio** is good at baseball. He has foot pain, but he is strong."

"I don't want to see sharks. Sharks will give us a hard time."

"Would **DiMaggio** stay with this fish?" he thought. "I think so. He is young and strong. Also his father was a fisherman."

Chapter 16
Arm Wrestling

It was sunset. He remembered the past. He remembered when he was arm-wrestling with a black man.

They wrestled all day. People went in and out of the room. He looked at the black man's arm and face.

Blood came from their hands. They looked at each other. People watched them. The people sat on chairs. There were blue walls. There were shadows on the walls.

There was no winner all night. The black man drank some

beer. The old man's hand was almost down. But the old man raised his hand.

The morning came. They were still in the game. The people wanted the game to end. Just then, the old man won the game.

The game started on a Sunday. The game ended on a Monday. People had to go to work soon. But the old man finished the game.

Everyone said he was "The Champion." There was a return game. But he won the game again.

He finished the games. The games were not good for his right hand. The right hand was for fishing. He played with his left hand. His left hand was bad. He lost the game.

"My hands will be warm in the sun," he thought. "I have to

stay warm."

An airplane flew overhead. Many flying fish jumped up. He pulled the fishing line. The fishing line did not move. The boat moved slowly.

"What does it feel like to be in an airplane?" he thought. "It must be strange. Maybe people in the airplane can see the fish in the water."

"I was on the top of the boat. I saw many fish. The dolphins looked green. Why are the fast fish purple? The dolphins are purple when they are hungry. I don't know why."

Chapter 17
The Dolphin

It was almost dark. The boat passed by a yellow sea plant. The yellow sea plant looked like a big island.

A dolphin was caught in the fishing line. The dolphin moved and jumped in the air. The old man pulled the dolphin in.

The old man pulled the fish into the boat. The fish hit the boat. The old man hit the fish with a club.

The old man unhooked the fish. He washed his left hand.

He held the fishing line with his left hand. He washed his right hand. He watched the sun go down.

"The fish is still going," he said.
His boat slowed down.
"The fish will slow down tomorrow," he thought.
"I will eat the dolphin later," he thought. "I will take a rest."

The old man dried his hand. He held the fishing line. He leaned on the boat.

"Fish! You did not eat anything," he said. "I ate tuna. And I had a dolphin."
"How do you feel, fish?" he asked. "I feel good. I have food."

He did not truly feel good. He still felt pain.
"It is okay. Bad things happened before," he thought.

"I have a cut on my hand. But my legs are fine, and I have food too."

It was dark. He rested in the boat. There was a star in the sky. More stars were coming out soon. The stars were his friends.

"The fish is my friend, too," he said. "You are an amazing fish. But I will kill you. I am glad people do not have to kill the stars."

"What if we went fishing for the moon?" he thought. "This is very strange. We don't have to kill the moon. I am glad."

"I need to think. I need to slow down the boat," he thought. "If the boat moves slowly, I may lose the fish. If the boat moves fast, it will be difficult."

"I will rest for one hour," he thought. "Then I will move. The fish is amazing. The hook was in the fish. But the fish is okay. The fish is hungry. I will rest."

Chapter 18
Sleep

The old man rested. 2 hours went by. The moon came out later. He did not know the time. The old man rested a little bit. The old man held the fishing line. It was hard.

"I want to tie the fishing line," he thought. "But I have to hold the fishing line."

"But I did not sleep," he said. "I did not sleep for two days. I need to sleep. I might get sick."

"My head is okay," he thought. "But I need to sleep. The moon sleeps. The sun sleeps. The ocean sleeps. I need to sleep."

"Now I will go back and prepare the dolphin."
He went to the back of the boat.

He held his knife. He pulled up the dolphin. He cut up the dolphin. He cleaned out the dolphin. There were two flying fish inside the dolphin. He skinned the dolphin.

He threw away the bones. He set down the dolphin. He set down the flying fish. He went to the front of the boat.

The old man set the fish on the wood. He moved the fishing line. He washed the flying fish in the water. His hand was dirty. He washed his hand.

"The fish is tired," the old man said. "Now I will eat some fish."
Under the stars, he ate the fish.

Dolphin is good to eat when it is cooked. But this time,

the dolphin was not cooked.

"I will have salt with me next time," he thought.

There were clouds in the sky. The old man looked at the clouds.

"There will be bad weather later," he thought. "But tonight will be okay. Get some sleep."

He held the fishing line in his right hand. He pushed on his right hand with his legs. He held the line in his left hand.

"My right hand can hold the fishing line," he thought. "If I let go, my left hand will help me. It is good to sleep."

He went to sleep.

Chapter 19
A Cut On the Hand

He dreamed of porpoises. The porpoises jumped. Then he dreamed of his bed. He was very cold. He rested on his right arm.

After that he dreamed of the yellow beach. He saw lions. He rested on the wood of the ship. The moon was in the sky. The old man slept.

The old man woke up. His hand hit his face. The fishing

line went into the water. He held the line again. The line burned his left hand.

The fish jumped. The fish jumped again. The boat was going fast. The old man held the fishing line. He fell down. He could not move.

"I waited for this," the old man thought. "I will make the fish work now."

The old man could hear the fish. The fishing line hurt his hands.

"I miss the boy," he thought.
The fishing line went out.

The old man was on his knees. He stood up. He felt the fishing line. He had more line in the boat.

"The fish jumped many times," he thought. "Now, the fish cannot swim deep in the water." Why is the fish scared? The fish was so strong. This is strange."

"Don't be afraid, old man," he said. "You cannot pull the line."

The old man held the line with his left hand. He washed his face. He watched the sun come up.

"The fish went to the east," he thought.

He looked at his right hand.
"It is not bad," he said.
He held the fishing line with his right hand. He put his left hand into the water.
"Well done," he said.

"I wish I had two good hands," he thought. "My left hand did well."

The old man was sick in the head. He needed to eat. He did not want to eat more dolphin. Then he remembered. He caught a flying fish.

He held the flying fish. He ate the flying fish.
"Now, I am strong," he thought. "I am ready."

Chapter 20
Circle

The old man was out at sea for three days. He could not see the fish. But he thought the fish was making a circle in the water. He pulled the fishing line. The fishing line came in.

He pulled in the line. He used his hands to pull the line. He used his body to pull the line.

"This is a very big circle," he said.

The fishing line stopped. The fishing line did not come into the boat. The fish pulled the line.

"The fish is making a big circle now," he said.

"I will hold the line," he thought. "Maybe I will see the fish in one hour."

But the fish swam for two more hours.

The old man saw black spots. Sweat was on his head. Sweat was in his eyes. He was not afraid of the black spots. But he felt sick.

"I can't die here," he said. "God, help me. I will pray one hundred times!"

The fishing line moved. The line felt heavy.

"The fish is hitting the fishing line," he thought. "Maybe the fish will jump."

"Don't jump, fish," he said.

The fish hit the line again. "I cannot pull too hard," the old man thought.

The fish swam in a circle. The fish pulled the line. The old man felt sick. He put water on his head.
"I have no cramps," he said. "The fish will come up."

The old man knelt down.
"I want to take a rest," he thought. "I will stand up when the fish is close to the boat."
The fish came close to the boat. The old man pulled the line.

"I am so tired," he thought.
The wind blew. The wind was good for the old man.
"I will rest," he said. "I feel good."

The old man sat down. He felt the fish moving.
"Swim fish, swim," he thought.
The wind was blowing.
"I can go home. I can find the way."

Chapter 21
The Death of the Marlin

He saw the fish. The fish was very big.
"Is that the fish? The fish is so big," he said.

That was the fish. It was that big. The fish swam up. The old man saw the tail on the fish. He saw the fish. The fish had a big body.

The old man could see the fish's eye. Two gray fish were there. They swam with the big fish. They were 90*cm* long.

The old man was sweating. He pulled the fishing line.
"I will put this harpoon in the fish soon," he thought.
"Be strong, old man," he said.

The fish turned again. The fish's back was up. It was time to catch the fish. The old man knew it. The harpoon was ready.

The fish was still swimming. The old man pulled the fishing line. The fish turned on its side.
"I made the fish turn over," the old man said.

The old man felt sick.
"Pull, hands! Work, legs! I will pull the fish in!" But the fish swam away.

"Fish, you will die," the old man said. "Do you have to kill me too?"
His mouth was too dry to speak.
"I want the fish to swim closer," he thought.

The fish swam away.
"You are killing me," the old man thought. "You are a great fish. You are a special fish. There is no fish like you." Come and kill me. I do not care."

"I don't know what to do," he thought. "I need to use my mind."
"Think! Think!" he said.

The fish swam around. The old man did not catch the fish. He felt sick. He tried again. Nothing changed.
"I will try one more time," he thought.

He tried. He could not catch the fish.

The old man pulled the fishing line. The fish came to the boat. Then the fish went past the boat.

The old man dropped the fishing line. He lifted his harpoon. He pushed his harpoon into the fish.

The fish jumped. Then it fell into the water.

The old man was sick. The fish turned over. Blood came out of the fish.

Chapter 22
Tying the Marlin to the Boat

"Be strong," he said to himself.
"I am tired. But I killed the fish. I have to work."

"I have to prepare the rope," he thought. "This fish is too big. I can't put it in the boat. I will tie the fish to the boat. Then I will go home."

He started to pull the fish in.
"I want to touch the fish," he thought. "I will bring the fish and tie it to the boat."

"Get to work, old man," he said.
The old man drank water.
"I have work to do."
He looked at the sky. It was afternoon. The wind blew.
"Come on, fish," he said.
The fish did not come. The old man went to the fish.

The old man saw the fish. The fish was very big. He untied the rope. The old man tied the fish to the boat. The fish was silver.

The old man felt better. He felt better because he drank water. His head was clear.
"The fish is 700 kilograms," he thought. "How much is it for

one kilo?'

"I need a pencil," he said.

He tied the fish tightly. The fish was so big. The fish was big like a boat. He cut a piece of line. He tied the fish's mouth. He set up the sail. He sailed southwest.

He knew where to go.

"I need food and water," he thought.

He got a yellow sea plant. He shook the yellow sea plant. Small shrimps fell onto the boat. He ate all of the shrimps. The shrimps were small, but they tasted good.

The old man had some water. The boat sailed on the ocean. He could see the fish. When he caught the fish, he thought it was a dream. But it was not a dream.

The old man knew. Everything was true. He looked at his hands.

"The hands will be good soon," he thought. "Salt water will help my hands."

"I have to keep my head clear."

The old man did not know what to do.

"Is the fish pulling me?"

"Maybe the fish is pulling me in."

Chapter 23
Mako Shark

The old man and the fish sailed together. The old man put his hands in the water. There were clouds in the sky. He kept looking at the fish. One hour later, a shark came.

The shark came up. The shark jumped out from the water. Then it followed the boat.

Sometimes the shark could not smell the fish. The shark smelled the fish again. It was a big **Mako** shark. The shark was beautiful. But it's mouth was not beautiful. The shark moved fast. It had many teeth. The shark had long teeth. The shark could eat many fish. Sharks are strong. Now the shark followed the boat.

The shark was coming. The shark was not scared. The old man prepared the harpoon. His head felt good. He looked at the fish. He watched the shark.
"I wish this was a dream," he thought.

The shark came to the boat. The old man saw the shark's teeth. The shark ate the fish. The old man put his harpoon into the shark's head.

The shark's eyes were dying. The shark's tail hit the water. The shark's body came up. Then it went down into the water.

"The shark ate about 20 kilograms of my fish," he said.

"The shark took my harpoon too," he thought.

He did not like to look at the fish.

"I killed the shark," he thought. "He was the biggest **Mako** shark."

"I wish it was a dream," he thought. "I wish I was in bed. I am sad. I killed the fish. This is a hard time. Sharks are smart and strong."

"Don't think, old man," he said. "Just keep going."

"But I must think," he thought. "Thinking is the only thing I can do."

"I killed the shark," he said to himself. "What would the great **DiMaggio** think? My hands were in pain. He has foot pain. Which one hurts more?"

"Think about something joyful," he said. "I'm getting closer to home. The boat became lighter."

"Aha!" he said. "I have a knife. I am an old man, but I have the knife."

The breeze was fresh. The old man sailed. He looked at the fish. He had hope.

"I killed the fish. Is that wrong?" he thought. "I'm not sure. I was born to be a fisherman. I was doing my job."

He liked to think. There was nothing to do. The old man thought for a long time.

"You didn't kill the fish to sell it," he thought. "You have pride. You are a fisherman."

"You think too much," he said.

"But you killed the shark," he thought.
"I killed the shark to save myself," the old man said.
"Everything kills something," he thought.

He took a bite of the fish. The fish tasted good. He wanted to sell the fish. But a hard time was coming.

Chapter 24
The Two Sharks

The wind blew. There were no other boats. He only saw flying fish.

He sailed for two hours. Sometimes he ate the fish. He saw a shark.
"Ay," he said.

"Shark," he said.
He saw two sharks. The sharks were **shovel-nosed** sharks.

He held the knife. He saw the sharks come up. He saw their heads and fins. They smelled bad. They wanted to eat.

"Ay," the old man said. "Come on sharks."
They came. One shark went under the boat. The other shark bit the fish. The old man put his knife in the shark's head. The shark fell down into the water.

The other shark came out from under the boat. The old man hit the shark with the knife. The shark was still alive. Then the shark came up again. He hit the shark's head. But the shark did not die.

"No?" the old man said.

He hit the shark again. Something broke. The shark was dead.

"Go. Go see your friend," he said.

The old man cleaned his knife.

Chapter 25
The Broken Knife

"The sharks ate so much of the fish," he said. "I wish it was a dream."

He did not want to look at the fish.

"I went out too far," he said. "Sharks will come again. I will prepare for the next time."

"I wish I had a stone for the knife," the old man said.

"You needed many things," he thought. "But you did not

bring them."

"You think too much," he said.

The old man put his hands in the water. The boat felt lighter. He did not want to think about the fish.

"It was a big fish," he thought. "Don't think of that. Just rest."

"What can I think about?" he thought.

"Nothing. Just wait for sharks."

"I wish it was a dream."

A shark came. The shark opened its mouth wide. The old man put his knife in the shark. But the knife broke.

The old man sailed the boat again. The shark was dead. The shark went down into the water.

"I have the gaff," he said. "But it will not help."

"I am too old to hit sharks," he thought.

He put his hands in the water. It was late in the day. He could not see the land. He wanted to see the land.

"You're tired," he said.

It was evening. The sharks were coming. They came to the boat.

He held the club with his right hand. He watched the sharks come. There were two sharks.

"I have to hit the shark's head," he thought.

The two sharks came close. He hit one shark on the head with a club. He hit the shark again.

The other shark came close. The old man hit it with a club. The shark looked at him. The old man hit the shark again.

"Come on, Shark," the old man said.

The shark swam up. The old man hit the shark. He felt the shark's bone. The shark moved away.

The old man waited for the sharks. But the sharks did not come. "I could not kill them," he thought. "But I did hurt them."

Chapter 26
Half of the Fish

Only half of the fish was there. He did not want to look.
"It will be dark soon," he said. "I will see the city lights."

"I will arrive soon," he thought. "The boy will be worried. Fishermen will be worried too. I live in a good town."

The fish was torn up.
"Half fish," he said. "I am sorry I came too far. But we killed many sharks."

"What will you do if the sharks come in the night?" he thought.
"Fight them," he said. "I will fight them until I die."

It was night time. There was no light. The old man felt like he was dead. He put his hands together. He felt pain. He was alive.

"I promised to pray," he thought. "But I am too tired. I have half of the fish. I wish I could bring the fish home."
"I need luck," he said.

"I want to buy luck," he said.
"How can I buy luck? Can I buy luck with a harpoon?" he asked himself.

"I can't think about silly things. I want to see the light," he thought.

Chapter 27
The Last Fight

He saw the lights. These were city lights. He sailed to the lights.

"The sharks will come," he thought. "I don't have a harpoon. How do I fight?"

His body was sick.

"I hope I don't have to fight again," he thought.

The sharks came in the middle of the night. They came in a group. The old man hit the sharks. A shark took his club.

The sharks came together. They ate the fish. They came back to eat more.

One more shark came. This was the last shark. The shark ate the fish. The fish was gone.

The old man felt something in his mouth. It was blood. The old man spit it out.

The old man had lost. The sharks had won.

The boat was light. The old man sailed the boat to his home. The sharks came again. The old man did not think about the sharks.

"The boat is good," he thought. "The boat is not broken."
He saw the lights of the beach.

"The wind is our friend," he thought. "The sea is our friend. The sea is our enemy too. My bed is my friend."

He sailed into the port. The lights of the Terrace were out. Everyone was in bed. He tied up his boat.

He walked home. He looked back. Only fish bones were left.

He walked again. He fell down. He tried to get up. It was too hard to get up. He sat for a while. He watched the road.

He started to walk again. He sat down five times on the way home. He arrived at his small house. He lay down on his bed. He went to sleep.

Chapter 28
At Home

The boy came to the old man's house. The old man was asleep. The boy saw him.

The boy cried. He went out to buy coffee for the old man.

Many fishermen were looking at the old man's boat.
"How is he?" a fisherman asked the boy.
"Sleeping," the boy said. "Let him sleep more."

The boy went into the Terrace.
"I would like a can of coffee, please."
"Do you want anything else?"
"No, thank you."

The boy came back to the old man's house. The old man was still asleep. The boy waited a long time. Finally, the old man woke up.

"Drink this," the boy said.
The old man drank the coffee.
"I lost, **Manolin**," he said.
"No. You got the fish."

"Did they look for me?" the old man asked.
"Yes. Many people looked for you."
"The ocean is very big," the old man said. "I missed you.

What did you catch?"

"I caught one fish on the first day. I caught one fish on the second day. I caught two fish on the third day," the boy said.

"Very good."

"Now we will fish together."

"No. I am not lucky."

"I will bring the luck," the boy said.

"I caught two fish yesterday. We will fish together."

"We need a good knife. My knife broke," the old man said.

"I will prepare everything," the boy said. "Let your hands rest."

"I will care for my hands."

"Lie down, old man. I will bring food for you."

"Bring me the newspapers," the old man said.

"I will bring the food and newspapers," the boy said. "Rest well, old man."

The boy went out the door. He cried again. People were having a party at the Terrace. They saw the bones of the fish. The old man was at home. He was sleeping. The boy was with him. The old man was dreaming about the lions.

Level 2는 Level 1의 문장에서 핵심 정보가 추가 되었습니다.

Level 1 보다 한 단계 높은 단어로 바뀐 문장도 있습니다.

THE ORIGINAL TEXT

"Be patient, hand," he said. "I do this for you." I wish I could feed the fish, he thought. He is my brother. But I must kill him and keep strong to do it. Slowly and conscientiously he ate all of the wedge-shaped strips of fish. He straightened up, wiping his hand on his trousers.

LEVEL 2

"Hold on, hand," he said.
"This is for you."
He ate all of the fish.
He cleaned his hand.

The Old Man and the Sea

LEVEL 2

Chapter 1
The Old Man and the Boy

He was an old fisherman. He had not caught a fish for 84 days. In the first 40 days, a boy had been with him, but now the boy was on another boat. The boy's parents had told him that the old man was unlucky.

The boy was sad to see the old man's empty boat. The boy always went down to help him carry his fishing tools.

The old man was skinny. He had deep wrinkles on his neck. Brown age spots from sunlight were on his cheeks. His hands had deep, old scars from handling fish on the ropes.

His body was old except for his eyes. His eyes were blue.

"**Santiago**," the boy said to him. "I could go with you again. We've made some money."

"No. You're with a lucky boat. Stay with them," the old man said.

"But remember the last time. We caught some big fish."

"I remember," the old man said. "But you have to obey your papa."

"Yes, I must obey him," the boy said. "Can I treat you to a beer on the Terrace?"

"Why not?" the old man said. "Let's have a drink together."

They sat on the Terrace. Other fishermen were there. They were talking about the old man.

Chapter 2
Friendship

The successful fishermen of that day carried their big fish to the fish house. They waited for the ice truck to carry the fish to the market in **Havana**.

The other fishermen had caught sharks. They had moved the sharks to the shark factory on the other side of the bay. When the wind was in the east, a bad smell came from the shark factory. But today the wind blew back to the north, and there was no bad smell. It was pleasant and sunny on the Terrace.

"**Santiago**," the boy said.
"Yes," the old man said.
"Can I go out to get some small fish for you for tomorrow?"
"No. Thank you."
"I would like to help you in some way."
"You bought me a beer," the old man said.

"How old was I when you first took me in a boat?"
"You were five, and we caught a tough fish. Do you remember?"
"I remember the fishtail hitting the boat and the seat breaking, and you were hitting the fish."
"Can you really remember that? Or did I tell you?"
"I remember everything."

"If you were my boy, we would go fishing together..." he said. "But you are your parents' son."

"May I get some small fish?"
"I have mine left from today."
"Let me get four fresh ones."
"Just one will be fine," the old man said.
His hope had never gone.
"Two," the boy said.
"Two," the old man agreed. "You didn't steal them?"
"I bought these," the boy said.

"Thank you," the old man said.

He humbly accepted the boy's offer.

"Tomorrow will be a good day to catch fish," the old man said.

"Where are you going?" the boy asked.

"I will go far out and come in when the wind changes."

"I'll ask him to go far and catch fish," the boy said. "If you catch big fish, we can come to help you."

"He does not like to fish too far out."

"But he can't see far. So I'll tell him there are dolphin fish far out," the boy said.

"Are his eyes that bad?"

"He is almost blind."

"It is strange," the old man said. "He never went hunting for turtles. Hunting turtles tires the eyes."

"But you went hunting for turtles, and your eyes are good."

"I am a strange old man."

"But are you strong enough to catch a big fish?"

"I think so."

"Let us take the stuff home," the boy said.

They picked up the stuff from the boat. The old man carried the mast, and the boy carried the wooden box, the gaff, and the harpoon. It was not a good idea to leave stuff on the boat.

Chapter 3
The Shack

They walked up the road together to the old man's tiny house. The old man put the mast down against the wall. The boy put the box and the other things down.

The tiny house was made of royal palm trees, and in it, there was a bed, a table, one chair, and a place to cook food. On the brown walls, there were two pictures in color. The old man's clean shirt was on the shelf in the corner.

"What do you have to eat?" the boy asked.

"A pot of yellow rice with fish. Do you want some?"

"No, I will eat at home. Do you want me to make the fire?"

"No. I will make it later on, or I may eat cold rice."

There was no pot of yellow rice and fish, but they played pretend every day.

"85 is a lucky number," the old man said. "How would you like to see me catch a big fish?"

"I'll catch some small fish. Will you sit in the doorway?"

"Yes, I have yesterday's newspaper, and I will read about the baseball game."

The old man took the paper out from under the bed.

"**Perico** gave it to me," he explained.

"I'll be back when I have some small fish. I'll keep yours

and mine together on ice. When I come back you can tell me about the baseball game."

"The **New York Yankees** will win."

"But I am scared of the **Cleveland Indians**."

"Have faith in the **New York Yankees**, my son. Think of the great **DiMaggio**."

"You read it and tell me about it when I come back."

"Should we buy a lottery ticket? How about a ticket with the number 85?" the old man said. "Tomorrow is the 85th day."

"Sure."

"Can you find a ticket with the number 85?"

"I can order one. Keep warm, old man," the boy said. "Remember we are in September."

"This is the month when the great fish come," the old man said.

"I will go now to get the small fish," the boy said.

When the boy came back, the old man was sleeping in the chair. The sun was down. The boy took a blanket off the bed. The boy covered the old man with the blanket. The old man's shoulders and neck were still strong. But he was old. He was wearing a very old shirt. He didn't have shoes.

Chapter 4
The Baseball Game

The boy left him there, and when he came back, the old man was still sleeping.

"Wake up old man," the boy said.

The old man opened his eyes.

"What did you bring?" the old man asked.

"I brought some food. We are going to have some food," the boy said.

"I'm not very hungry."

"You can't go fishing without eating anything."

The old man got up and folded the newspaper. "What are we eating?"

"Black beans and rice, fried bananas, and some stew," the boy answered.

The boy brought the food from the Terrace. The boy also brought two forks and two spoons.

"Who gave this to you?"

"**Martin**. He owns the Terrace."

"I need to thank him."

"I thanked him already," the boy said. "You don't need to thank him."

"I will give him some part of a big fish," the old man said.

"He also gave us two beers."

"I like the beer in cans."

"I know, but this is in bottles. I will take back the bottles."
"That's very kind of you," the old man said.

"Should we eat?" the old man said.
"Yes, let's eat. I'll wait until you are ready to eat."
"I'm ready now," the old man said.

"Your stew is great," the old man said.
"Tell me about the baseball game," the boy asked him.
"The best baseball team is the **Yankees**," the old man said happily.
"But they lost today," the boy told him.
"That means nothing. The great **DiMaggio** is doing well again."
"They have other men on the **Yankees** team."
"Yes, but the great **DiMaggio** makes a difference," the old man said.
"What about the other baseball team?" the boy asked.
"There is the **Philadelphia** team, and they have **Dick Sisler**."

"Do you remember when **Dick Sisler** came here?"
"I wanted to take him fishing but I was too shy."
"And you were shy too."
"I know. It was a great mistake," the boy said. "If we asked him, maybe he would have gone with us."
"I would like to take the great **DiMaggio** fishing," the old man said.
"People say his father was a fisherman."

"The great Sisler's father was a baseball player."

"When he was a baseball player, I was in Africa," the old man said.

"I know. You told me."

"Tell me about the great **John J. McGraw**," the boy said.

"He came to the Terrace sometimes. But he drank too much beer. And he loved horse racing as well as baseball."

"He was a great manager," the boy said. "My father thinks he was the greatest."

"That's because he came here many times," the old man said.

"Who is the greatest manager, **Luque** or **Mike Gonzalez**?" the boy asked.

"I think they are both great."

"And the best fisherman is you."

"There are other fishermen who are better than me."

"No, you are the best."

"Thank you. You make me happy."

"You have to sleep now."

"Good night! I'll wake you up tomorrow morning."

"You're my alarm clock," the boy said.

"Age is my alarm clock," the old man said.

"Have a good sleep, old man."

"Good night."

Chapter 5
Going Fishing

The boy left. They ate the food in the dark. The old man took off his pants and went to bed.

He fell asleep quickly. He dreamed of when he was a boy. He dreamed of his time in Africa. He saw the golden beaches and the big brown mountains in the dream. He heard the waves. He smelled the deck of the ship. He also smelled the smell of Africa. Usually, when he smelled the smell of Africa in his dream, he woke up and got dressed. But tonight the smell came too early. So he stayed asleep and dreamed a longer dream. In his dream, he saw the mountains of the Canary Islands.

He no longer dreamed of storms, great fish, or his wife. He only dreamed of places and lions on the beach. He loved lions like he loved the boy. He woke up, and he looked at the moonlight outside the door. He put on his pants. He went to wake up the boy. The outside air was cold.

He went to the boy's house. The boy's house was unlocked. The boy was sleeping on a bed in the first room. The old man touched the boy's foot. The boy woke up and looked at him. The boy put on his pants. The old man went out and the boy came with him. The old man put his arm across the boy's shoulders.

"I am sorry," the old man said.
"No, it is what I have to do," the boy said.

They walked to the old man's tiny house. There were fishermen on the road. The fishermen walked to their boats. They came to the house with the fishing tools.
"Do you want coffee?" the boy asked.
"Let's put the tools in the boat and then get some."
They had coffee at the coffee shop.

"How did you sleep, old man?" the boy asked.
"Very well, **Manolin**," the old man said. "I feel good today."
"So do I," the boy said. "I'll get some small fish for you and me."

"Thank you," the old man said.
"I'll be right back," the boy said. "Have another coffee."

He walked to the ice house. The old man drank his coffee slowly. For a long time, he never carried his lunch box with him. He had only a bottle of water in the boat.

The boy came back with the small fish. They went down to the boat. They pushed the boat into the water.
"Good luck, old man."
"Good luck," the old man said.
He began to row in the dark. There were other boats going out to sea. The old man heard the sound of the boats moving.

Chapter 6
Bait

Sometimes someone in a boat would talk. But most of the boats were silent. They sailed through the harbor to the ocean. They hoped to find fish. The old man rowed out. He wanted to go far out.

He rowed over to one part of the ocean. He saw the light of the Gulf weed in the water. There was a hole there. The fishermen called the hole, **"the great well."** It was 1,260 meters deep. There were many kinds of fish there. Shrimp and squid came close to the surface at night.

The old man could feel the morning coming. He heard the flying fish. He liked the flying fish. The flying fish were his good friends.

The old man was sorry for the small birds. The small birds were always flying to find fish. He thought that the birds had a hard time. Why were the birds so weak? The small birds were too weak to live on the sea.

The old man always thought of the sea as a lovely woman. Sometimes people say bad things about the sea. Some of the younger fishermen had motorboats. They thought of the sea as a man. Sometimes the sea was wild. But the old man always thought of the sea as a woman.

He was rowing along and it was not hard for him. The sea was calm. Daylight was coming. He saw that he was further out than he thought.

He thought, "I fished for one week. I did not catch any fish. Today I'll go to where the schools of tuna are."

He threw his baits out into the water before it was light. One bait was down 72 meters. The second one was down 135 meters. The third and fourth ones were down 180 and 225 meters. The baits were head down with the hooks. The points of the hooks were covered with fresh small fish. The hooks were filled with sweet-smelling fish.

The boy gave him two small tunas. The tunas hung on the two deepest fishing lines. The old man hung a blue fish and a yellow fish on the other fishing lines. The lines were thick like a big pencil. There was a green stick with the fishing lines. Each fishing line had enough string to go far.

Now the old man watched the three sticks. He rowed softly. He kept the lines straight. Light was coming. The sun rose up. The old man could see the other boats. The sun was very bright and a strong light came on the water. As the sun came up, his eyes hurt. He rowed his boat. He did not look at the sun.

He watched the fishing lines. The lines went straight down into the dark water. He kept the lines very straight. He kept the lines at the right depth.

He thought, "I have no luck. But who knows? Maybe today is the day."

Chapter 7
A Man-Of-War Bird

The sun had come up. Two hours went by. There were only three boats in sight. They were close to the beach.
He thought, "The morning sun always hurts my eyes. But I can look straight into the evening sun."

Just then, he saw a **man-of-war bird**. The bird was flying in a circle in the sky.

"He's got something," the old man said aloud. "He's not just looking."

He rowed toward the bird. He did not hurry. He kept his lines straight up and down.

The bird flew higher. The bird flew in a circle again. Then the bird came down quickly. The old man saw flying fish.

"Dolphin," the old man said aloud. "Big dolphin."

He brought a small fishing line. The line had a hook. The hook was a medium size. He threw the line over the side. Then he prepared another fishing line. He was rowing again, and he was watching the **man-of-war bird**.

The bird came down again. The bird tried to catch the flying fish. The old man saw the dolphin following the flying fish.

He thought, "It is a big school of dolphins. They're going to get the flying fish."

He watched the flying fish and the bird again.

"The flying fish are moving away from me," he thought. "They are moving out too fast. But maybe I will catch a fish behind them."

The clouds went up over the land like mountains. The coast was like a long green line. The water was a blue color. The blue color was almost purple. He saw the plankton in the dark water. He was happy to see the plankton. This meant that fish were there.

The sun came up higher. The clouds came up over the land. The weather was good. But the bird was far away. The bird was hard to see. There was nothing around. There was only a big purple jellyfish. The jellyfish had poison in it.

"This is bad water," the old man said. "You are sneaky."

He looked down into the water. He saw the tiny purple fish. The tiny fish swam between the jellyfish. They were strong. They were not hurt by the poison from the jellyfish. But humans were not strong enough. Sometimes the jellyfish poison hurt the old man's hands.

The jellyfish had beautiful colors. But they were dangerous. The old man loved to see the sea turtles eating the jellyfish. The turtles ate them all. The old man also loved to walk on them on the beach.

He loved **green turtles** and **hawk-bill turtles**. They were fast. They had style. He didn't like **loggerhead turtles** with yellow shells.

He had hunted turtles for many years. Some turtles were as long as a boat. They were very heavy. He was sorry for them all. Most people do not care about turtles.

But the old man thought, "The turtles and I are no different."

Chapter 8
Albacore

Now the old man looked up. The bird was flying in a circle again.

"The bird found fish," he said.

There was no flying fish. But the old man watched the sea. A small tuna jumped out of the water. More and more tuna jumped up. Then the tuna jumped from all directions.

He thought, "If they are not too fast, I can catch up."
He watched the group of tuna and the bird.

"The bird is a great help," the old man said.

Just then the fishing line moved. He caught the fishing line. The he pulled it up. It was a small tuna. The back of the tuna was blue. The tuna lay in the boat. The tuna's tail moved quickly. The old man hit the tuna on the head.

"This is **Albacore**," he said out loud. "It will be good for bait. It will weigh 4.5 kilograms."

He did not know when he started talking to himself.

Maybe the old man started to talk out loud when the boy left. The old man and the boy did not talk together very much.

"If the others heard me talking out loud to myself, they

would think that I am crazy," he said. "But I am not crazy. I do not care."

"Now is the time to think of one thing," he thought. "I will think about fishing. Maybe a big fish is here. I picked up only one tuna. The fish I saw today moved quickly. It went to the northeast. Is the weather strange today? I do not know."

Now he could not see the green coast. He could only see the tops of the hills. The clouds looked like high mountains. The sea was very dark. The light made shapes in the water. The old man saw the deep blue sea. He saw his fishing lines in the water.

Chapter 9
Encounter

The tunas were gone. The fishermen called many kinds of fish "tuna." The sun was hot. The old man felt the sun on the back of his neck.

"I could sleep a little," the old man thought. "But I should catch a big fish."

Just then, he saw the green stick go down into the water.
"Yes," he said. "Yes."

He held the fishing line lightly. He did not feel anything. A little later, he felt something. A fish gently pulled the fishing line.

The old man held the line softly. He untied the line from the stick with his left hand.

"This fish must be huge," he thought. "Eat the baits, fish.

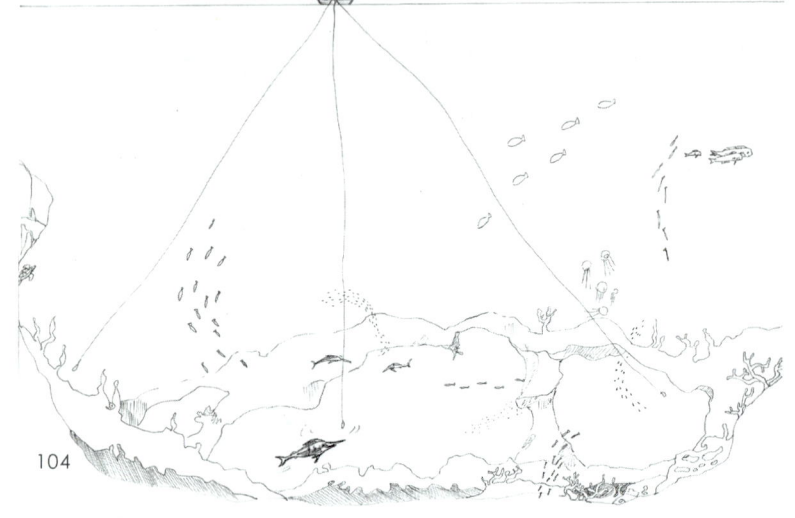

Eat them. Please eat them. They are so fresh!"

He felt light pulling and then stronger pulling. Then there was nothing.

"Come on," the old man shouted. "Turn around. Just smell them. Aren't they great? Don't be shy, fish. Eat them."

He waited. He held the fishing line and watched it. Then he felt the pulling again.

"The fish will take the bait this time," the old man said aloud. "God, help the fish to eat it."

But the fish did not eat it. The fish was gone. The old man felt nothing.

"The fish didn't go away," he said. "The fish is turning."

Then he felt the little touch on the fishing line. He was happy.

"The fish just moved," he said. "The fish will eat it."

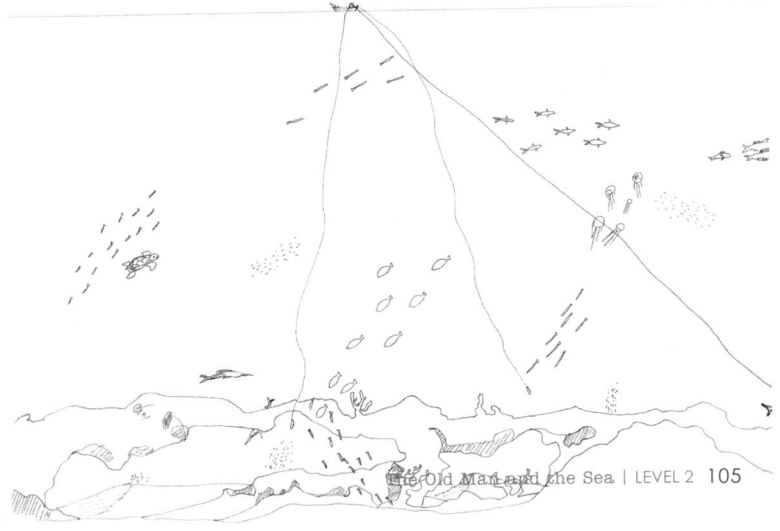

He was happy to feel the pull of the fishing line. He felt something strong and heavy. It was the large fish. He let the line slip down. The fishing line went down. He used extra fishing lines. He could feel the big fish as it went down.

"What a fish," he said. "The fish is going away with the bait."
"The fish will eat the bait," he thought.
He knew it was a big fish. He felt the fish stop. But the line was heavy. He put out more fishing line. The fishing line went down.

"The fish took the bait," he said. "Now I will let the fish eat."
He let the line go through his fingers. He prepared extra fishing lines. Now he was ready. He had 3 bundles of lines. They were 72 meters long.

"Eat it a little more," he said. "Enjoy."
"Eat it! Then the hook will go into your heart and kill you," he thought. "All right. Are you ready?"
"Now!" he said aloud.
He pulled up one meter of fishing line with his hands. He pulled the line again and again.

Nothing happened. The fish moved slowly away. The old man could not bring up the fish. His fishing line was strong. The line was for heavy fish. The old man held the line. The boat moved slowly.

The fish moved ahead. The boat moved slowly. The other

baits were still in the water.

"I wish the boy was here with me," the old man said. "The fish is pulling this boat. I could tie the fishing line to the boat. But the fish could break the line. I have to hold on. I am thankful the fish is not going down."

He held the line against his back. He watched the line. The boat was moving.

"If the fish keeps moving the boat, the fish will die," the old man thought.

But the fish kept swimming.

"It was noon when I caught the fish," the old man said. "But I have not seen the fish."

He put on his hat too tightly. His hat hurt his forehead. He was thirsty too. He found his water bottle. He opened the water bottle. He drank a little bit of water.

Then he looked behind him. He could not see any land.

"It will be dark in two hours. The fish will come up before dark," he thought. "My hands are fine and I feel strong. The fish has the hook in its mouth. The hook must hurt the fish."

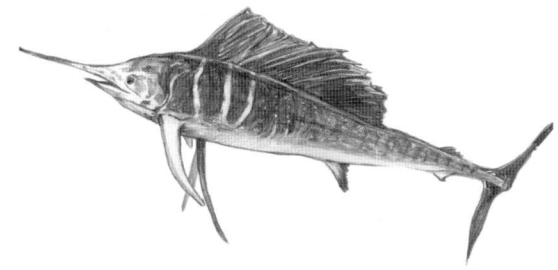

Chapter 10
Moving Along

The old man looked at the sky. There were stars. He watched the stars. He could tell where the boat was. The sun went down and it was cold. There was a sack. The old man put the sack on his back. The sack became a cushion for the old man and the fishing line.

"There's nothing I can do with the fish," he thought.

He stood up. He looked at the stars and checked his course. The boat was moving slowly. The light of the land was not strong. The boat was going east.

"If I can't see the light of the land, we are going east," he thought.

"What happened at the baseball game today?" he wondered.

But he had to focus on fishing.

"I wish the boy were here. I wish he could help me. I wish he could see this fish," he said out loud.

"I must remember to eat the tuna tomorrow. I need to keep strong," he said to himself.

During the night, two dolphins followed the boat.

"They are good. They are our brothers like the flying fish," he said.

He thought of the big fish. He felt sad for the big fish.

"How old is this fish? I never had a strong fish like this. This fish is not wild. This is very strange," he thought. "The fish does not know that I'm alone. The fish has no fear. What a great fish."

The old man remembered the past. There were two marlin fish. One was a male. The other was a female. The male fish gave food to the female fish first. The old man caught the female fish. The male fish had stayed with the female fish.

The old man held the head of the female fish. The old man hit the female fish with a club. The old man put the female fish on the boat. The male fish waited by the boat. The old man prepared the harpoon. The male fish jumped. Then the male fish went away.

"The male fish was wonderful," the old man remembered.

"I wish the boy were here," he said out loud.

He leaned against the front of the boat. He felt the weight of the fish.

"You made a choice, fish. You chose to stay in the water. I chose to go there to find you. There is no one to help us. I was born for this job. I'm a fisherman," the old man thought.

Chapter 11
Tug-of-war

Something took one of the baits. The fishing line kept going into the water. It was still dark. The old man took out his knife. He cut the fishing lines. He tied the lines together. He worked with one hand. He had six extra fishing lines.

"I will cut the rest of the line and tie it up," he thought. "I lost 360 meters of good fishing line. That can be replaced. But what if I lose this big fish? How could I replace this fish? What was that other fish? A marlin or a shark? I never felt that fish."

"I wish the boy were here," he said out loud.
"But the boy is not here. You are alone. You need to work," he thought.
He cut the fishing lines. He tied the fishing lines. The big fish moved fast. The old man fell down. He hurt his face. He rested against the boat.

He moved the fishing line. He felt the fish pull the line. He put his hand into the water. He felt the speed of the boat.

"Why did the fish move fast?" he thought. "Maybe something hurt the fish. But I have pain in my back. The fish cannot pull this boat forever. Now everything is fine."

"Fish," he said softly. "I'll stay with you until the end."

"The fish will stay with me too," the old man thought.

It was cold because it was still dark. He waited for the sun to come up.

"I can do it as long as the fish can," he thought.

The boat kept moving. The sun came up. The fishing line was on the old man's shoulder.

"He's moving north," the old man said.

"The waves are moving us to the east," he thought. "I wish the fish would get tired."

The sun went up a little higher. There was one good sign. The fish was swimming up a little.

"God, let the fish jump," the old man said. "I have enough line to handle the fish."

"I can pull the fishing line. Maybe the fish will jump up," he thought.

He tried to pull the fishing line. But the line couldn't move.

"I will not pull the fishing line," he thought. "If I pull it, the hook will become loose. The hook might come off. Anyway, I feel good. I don't have to look at the sun."

There was yellow seaweed on the fishing line. The yellow seaweed made light when it was night time.

"Fish," he said.

"I love you, but I will kill you," he thought.

Chapter 12
A Small Bird

A small bird came toward the boat. The old man could see that the bird was very tired. The bird sat in the front of the boat. Then the bird flew to the fishing line.

"How old are you?" the old man asked the bird. "Is this your first trip?"

When he spoke, the bird looked at him.

"This fishing line is steady," the old man said to the bird. "What happened to you? Why are you so tired?"

"Big birds will hurt these little birds later," he thought.

"Take a good rest, small bird," he said. "Then go and take your chance. Stay at my house if you want to. I'm sorry I can't take you back. I am with a big fish."

The fish moved very fast. The old man fell down in the boat. The fishing line moved. The bird flew away.

He felt the line with his hand. His right hand was bleeding.
"Something hurt the fish," he said out loud.
He pulled on the fishing line. But the line was tight.

"You're feeling it now," he said to the fish. "I am feeling it too."

He looked for the bird. The bird was gone.

"I fell down fast. How did that happen?" he thought. "I was looking at the small bird. I was busy thinking. Now I will think about work. I need to eat the tuna."

"I wish the boy were here," he said out loud.

Chapter 13
Left Hand

The old man got down on his knees. He washed his hand in the ocean. The blood washed away. He watched the movement of the water.

"The fish is going slowly," he said.

The old man wanted to keep his hand in the water. He stood up and held up his hand. There was a cut, but it was not deep. The old man was mad because he hurt his hand. He needed his hand to do his work.

"I will eat the small tuna," he said.

He found the tuna in the boat. He held the fishing line. He put his knee on the tuna. He cut the tuna into six pieces.

"I don't think I can eat all of this," he said.

The old man cut the piece of fish in two. His left hand felt strange. His left hand couldn't move. His left hand was cramped.

"What is wrong with my hand?" he said. "I have a cramp. Oh no."

"Eat the tuna now," he thought. "Your hand is working hard. Your hand is tired."

He put a little chunk of fish in his mouth. He ate it.

"I wish I had lemon or salt," he thought.

"How do you feel, hand?" he asked his hand.
The cramp was very bad. His hand was stiff.
"I'll eat more fish for you."
He ate the other piece of fish. He ate it slowly.
"How are you, hand?" the old man asked.
He ate another piece.

"The tuna is a strong and healthy fish," he thought. "I am happy I do not have a dolphin. I am happy with this tuna fish. Dolphin is not good to eat. I have no salt. I can't dry the tuna fish. I am not hungry now, but I will eat the tuna."

"Hold on, hand," he said. "This is for you."
He ate all of the fish. He cleaned his hand.

"Hand, you can let the fishing line go," he said. "I will hold the line with just my right arm."

"God, make the cramp go away," he said. "I don't know what the fish is going to do."
"The fish is quiet," he thought. "What is the fish's plan? If the fish jumps, I can kill it. If the fish stays down for a long time, I will stay down for a long time."

He rubbed his hand against his pants. But his hand would not open up.
"Maybe my hand will open in the afternoon," he thought. "I will let it open by itself. I do not want to push it to open. I used this hand too much yesterday."

Chapter 14
Jumping Up

He knew he was very alone now. But he could see beautiful shapes in the water. The clouds were getting bigger. He saw wild ducks in the sky. The wild ducks flew high over the water. No other man was alone on the sea like him.

"Some people are scared to go far out in a small boat," he thought. "Sometimes, there is bad weather. The weather changes fast. But if there are no big storms, the weather is good."

You can see big storms on the sea. But, this is hard to see on the land. The land is different.

He looked at the sky. The clouds looked like ice cream. "This is a good breeze," he said. "This is a great day."

His left hand was still cramped. But it was getting better.
"I hate cramps," he thought. "My own body is causing trouble. Cramps make me feel bad."

"If the boy were here, he could rub my hand," he thought.

The fishing line felt different. He saw the line moving in the water. He hit his hand.

"The fish is coming up," he said.

The fishing line came up slowly. The surface of the ocean splashed. The fish came out. The fish was bright. His head and back were dark purple. His sword was long. The fish went back into the water. The old man saw the big tail of the fish.

"The fish is longer than the boat," the old man said.

The fishing line went down fast. The old man was trying to hold the fishing line. The old man used both hands.

"This is a big fish. I must catch it," he thought. "The fish does not know that he is strong. I'm glad the fish does not know. I'm glad the fish does not swim too fast."

The old man saw many big fish. He caught very heavy fish. This was the first time that he met a big fish alone. His left hand still had a cramp.

"My hand will feel better," he thought. "It will help my right hand. The fish are brothers. My two hands are brothers." The fish moved slowly again.

"I wonder why the fish jumped," the old man thought. "Now, I know how big he is."

"I wish I could show him who I am," he thought. "The fish thinks I am strong."

Chapter 15
The Prayer

The old man rested in the boat. The fish moved ahead. The boat moved slowly. The wind blew. There was a small wave on the sea. At noon, the old man's hand felt good. There was no cramp.

"Bad news for you, fish," he said.
He felt good, but he was still in pain.
"I don't have much faith," he said.
"But I will say a prayer ten times."
"If I catch this fish, I will go to church."
"I promise."

He began to pray. He was so tired. He could not remember the prayer. But he kept praying.

The old man finished his prayer. He felt better but he was in pain. He rested in the boat. He began to move the fingers of his left hand. The sun was hot. The breeze was softly blowing.

"I have no more food. I will catch another fish. I think I can catch a dolphin. But I want to catch a flying fish. Flying fish taste so good. I don't need to cut the fish," he said. "This fish is too big. I will kill it."
"I will show the fish what a man can do," he thought.

"I told the boy that I was a strange old man," he said. "Now I will prove it."

He proved it many times. But it didn't matter. Each time was a new time. Now he had to prove it.

"I want the fish to fall asleep. I want to sleep and dream about lions. Why do I dream of lions?" he thought.

"Do not think, old man," he said to himself. "Take a rest in the boat."

Then, it was afternoon. The boat moved along slowly. But there was a breeze from the east. The boat was heavy. The fish slowed down. The old man's back felt better.

Once in the afternoon, the fishing line came up again. But the fish did not jump again. The sun was on the old man's left arm. He knew the fish turned to the east.

The old man saw the fish once. He thought of the fish swimming with his wide fins.

"Big eyes help the fish to see in the dark. The fish has big eyes. The fish's eyes are bigger than a horse's eyes. The horse can see in the dark. How well can the fish see in the dark?" he thought.

His left hand felt better. He kept moving. The left hand began to help the right hand.

"If you are not tired, fish," he said out loud. "You are very strange."

He felt very tired. He knew the night would come. He tried to think of other things. He thought of baseball games. He knew there was a baseball game.

"I don't know who won the baseball game," he thought. "But I must have faith in the great **DiMaggio**. He is very good at baseball, even with his foot pain."

"I hope there are no sharks. If there are sharks, it will be dangerous," he said out loud.

"Would the great **DiMaggio** stay with this fish for a long time?" he thought. "I think so. He is young and strong. Also his father was a fisherman."

Chapter 16
Arm Wrestling

It was sunset. He remembered the past when he was in a bar. He remembered when he was arm-wrestling with a black man.

They arm wrestled each other. They wrestled one day and one night. Each one was trying to win. People went in and out of the room. He looked at the black man's arm and face.

Blood came from their fingernails. They looked at their eyes and hands. People went in and out of the room. They sat on high chairs. The walls were painted blue. There were shadows on the walls.

There was no winner all night. People gave some beer to the black man. The black man tried hard. The old man's hand was almost down on the table. But the old man raised his hand again. The old man was sure he could win.

The morning came. They were still fighting. The people wanted to stop the game. The old man suddenly pushed the black man's hand down.

The game started on a Sunday morning. The game ended

on a Monday morning. People wanted to stop the game because they had to go to work soon.

But the old man finished the game.

He was called "The Champion" for a long time after that. There was a return game. He won the game again.

After that, he played a few games. Then he finished playing games. Games were bad for his right hand. The right hand was important for fishing. He played with his left hand. But his left hand was not good. He lost every game.

"The sun will warm my hands," he thought. "I don't want to get a cramp again. I have to stay warm in the night."

An airplane flew overhead. The old man watched the airplane's shadow. Many flying fish jumped up.

"I see flying fish, so dolphins must be here too," he said.

He pulled the fishing line. The fishing line did not move. The boat moved slowly.

"I wonder what it feels like to fly in an airplane," he thought. "It must be very strange in an airplane. Maybe people in the airplane can see the fish well. I want to see the fish from up there."

"When I was on the turtle boat, I was on the top of the boat. I saw many fish. The dolphins looked more green from up there. I could see a school of fish. Why do the fast fish have purple backs and purple spots? The dolphin looks green. But when the dolphin is hungry, it turns purple. I don't know why."

Chapter 17
The Dolphin

It was almost dark. The boat passed by some yellow seaweed. The yellow seaweed looked like a big island. The yellow seaweed moved up and down.

A dolphin was caught in the fishing line. The dolphin jumped in the air. It looked like gold in the sun. The fish was afraid, and it jumped again. The old man pulled the dolphin in with his left hand.

When the fish was near the boat, he pulled the fish into the boat. The fish had a long body. The fish hit the boat with its body. The old man hit the fish with a club.

The old man unhooked the fish. He put the bait on the fishing line. He threw the line into the sea. He washed his left hand in the sea. Then he moved the fishing line to his left hand. He washed his right hand in the sea. He watched the sun go down.

"The fish hasn't changed at all," he said.

His boat slowed down.

"Tomorrow, the fish will slow down," he said. "Have a good night, fish."

"It would be better to eat a little later," he thought. "I will take a rest for now."

His hand dried in the air. He held the fishing line with his right hand. He relaxed and leaned forward against the boat.

"Fish! You did not eat anything," he said. "I ate all the tuna. And I had a dolphin. I will eat the dolphin tomorrow."

"How do you feel, fish?" he asked out loud. "I feel good and I have food. Pull the boat, fish."

He did not really feel good. He was still in pain.

"It is okay. Bad things happened before," he thought. "My hand has a little cut. The cramp is gone from my hand. My legs are fine. I have food too."

It was dark. It was September. The sun set early. He rested in the front of the boat. There was a star in the sky. He did not know the name of the star. Other stars would come out soon. The stars were his friends.

"The fish is my friend, too," he said out loud. "You are an amazing fish. But I must kill you. I am glad people do not have to kill the stars."

"What if people had to kill the moon?" he thought. "The moon runs away. It is good that we do not have to try to kill the moon."

"I need to think about slowing down the boat," he thought. "This was a good idea. This was also a bad idea. If the boat slows down, I may lose the fish. But if the boat doesn't slow down, it will be difficult. I need to eat the dolphin now."

"I will rest for one hour," he thought. "Then I will move. It is good to slow down. I need to think about safety. The fish is amazing. I saw the hook in the fish's mouth. The fish is okay with the hook in its mouth. But the fish is very hungry. This is difficult for the fish. I will rest now."

Chapter 18
Sleep

He rested for almost 2 hours. The moon rose later. He did not know the time. He tried to rest. He held the fishing line. It was difficult.

"I wish I could tie the fishing line. But the line might break," he thought. "I have to support the fishing line."

"But you haven't slept yet," he said out loud. "You haven't slept for almost two days. Think of a way to sleep. If you don't sleep, you will get sick in the head."

"My head is fine," he thought. "I am bright like the stars. But I need to sleep. The moon and the sun sleep too. I can't forget to sleep. I need to take care of the fishing line."

"Now I will go back and prepare the dolphin."
He went to the back of the boat. He thought he might be half asleep.

The old man was in the back of the boat. He held his knife. The stars were bright. He saw the dolphin. He pulled up the dolphin. He put his feet on the fish and cut it up. He cleaned out the inside. There were two flying fish inside the dolphin. He threw the other parts away. He skinned the dolphin.

He threw away the bones of the dolphin. He looked in the water. He set down the flying fish and the dolphin. He put his knife away. He went to the front of the boat.

The old man set the fish on the wood with the flying fish. He put the fishing line in a new place. He held the line with his left hand. He washed the flying fish in the water. His hand was dirty. He watched the water. The boat moved slowly.

"The fish is tired," the old man said. "Let me eat some fish and get some rest."
Under the stars, he ate the dolphin and the flying fish.

Dolphin is good to eat when it is cooked. But it is bad to eat when it is uncooked.
"Next time, I will bring salt in the boat," he said. "This was my mistake."

The sky was cloudy. The stars were gone. He saw the clouds in the sky.
"There will be bad weather," he thought. "But not tonight. Get some sleep, old man."

He held the fishing line in his right hand. He pushed on his right hand with his leg.
He leaned on the boat. He held the line with his left hand.

"My right hand can hold the fishing line," he thought. "If I let go, my left hand will wake me up. If I sleep for a little

bit, it is good."
He went to sleep.

Chapter 19
A Cut On the Hand

He did not dream of the lion. He dreamed of porpoises. The porpoises jumped up in the air. He dreamed that he was on his bed. There was a north wind. He was very cold. He rested on his right arm.

The old man had a dream again. He saw the yellow beach. He saw lions. The first lion came down to the beach. The other lions followed. He rested on the wood of the ship. He felt the breeze. He waited for more lions. The moon came out. The old man was still sleeping.

The old man woke up. His right hand hit his face. The fishing line slipped out of his hand. He had no feeling in his hand. The line went out of his hand. He held the line again with his left hand. He leaned back. The line burned his left hand and his back.

He looked back at the extra fishing line. Just then, the fish jumped up and fell down. The fish jumped again and again. The boat was going fast. The line was still going out. The old man held the fishing line. The line pulled the old man down. He fell on his face. His face was on the piece of dolphin. He could not move.

"I waited for this," the old man thought. "I will make the fish work hard."

He could not see the fish. He heard the fish splashing. The line was moving fast. The line cut his hands. He did not want the line to hurt his fingers.

"If the boy were here, he would get the fishing line wet for me," he thought. "I wish he was here."

The fishing line went out.

He lifted his head. He lifted his head out of the piece of dolphin. He was on his knees. He stood up slowly. He felt the extra fishing line with his feet. There was a lot of line.

"The fish jumped more than ten times," he thought. "The fish has a sack on his back. The sack is full of air. The fish can't swim deep in the water. The fish can't swim away and die. The fish will go in a circle. Why is the fish scared? The fish was so strong. This is strange."

"Don't be afraid, old man," he said. "You cannot pull the line."

The old man held the line with his left hand. He bent down. He washed his face with his right hand.

The old man washed his face. He watched the sun rise.

"The fish was going to the east," he thought. "The fish is tired."

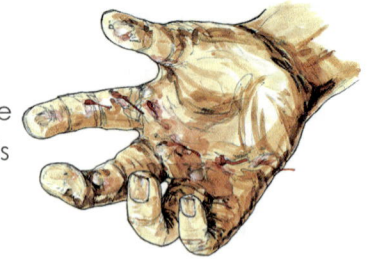

He looked at his right hand.

"It is not bad," he said. The pain is okay for me. I am strong."

He held the fishing line with his right hand. He put his left hand into the water.

"You did a good job," he said.

"I don't have two good hands. Why?" he thought. "My left hand did well. My left hand had one cramp."

The old man felt sick in his head. He thought he should chew on the dolphin. But he didn't want to eat the dolphin. He remembered the flying fish in the boat.

There was the flying fish. It was clean. The old man held the flying fish. He ate it.

"The flying fish is good to eat," he thought. "This fish will make me strong. I'm ready."

Chapter 20
Circle

It was the third day on the ocean. The old man did not see the fish swimming. But he thought the fish was swimming in a circle. He pulled the fishing line with his right hand. The fishing line came in slowly.

He started to pull in the line slowly. He used both of his hands. He tried to pull with his body too.

"This is a very big circle," he said.
Then the fishing line would not come in anymore. He held the line. The fish pulled the line.

"The fish is making a big circle now," he said.
"I have to hold the line," he thought. "Maybe I will see the fish in one hour."
But the fish swam for two more hours. The old man was wet with sweat. He was very tired. But then, the fish swam in small circles.

The old man saw black spots for one hour. Sweat was on his face. His eyes hurt from the salt in the sweat. The cut on his head hurt. He was not afraid of the black spots. He knew he would see black spots. But he felt dizzy. He was worried.

"I can't fail. I can't just die here," he said. "The fish is coming up. God, help me. I will pray to you one hundred times!"

He felt the line move quickly. The line felt very heavy.

"The fish is hitting the fishing line with his sharp nose. I knew it. Maybe the fish will jump. I want the fish to keep swimming."

"Don't jump, fish," he said.

The fish hit the line again. "I can't pull too hard," he thought. "I can't give the fish more pain."

The fish swam in a circle again. The fish pulled on the line. The old man felt dizzy again. He put some water on his head. "I have no cramps," he said. "The fish will come up."

The old man knelt down for a moment.
"I will rest now. The fish will swim in a circle," he thought. "I will stand up when the fish comes close to the boat."
The old man wanted to rest. The fish came close to the boat. The old man stood up and pulled the line.

"I am very tired," he thought.
The wind started blowing. The wind was good for the old man.
"I will rest when the fish swims," he said. "I feel very good."

The old man sat down with the fishing line. He felt the fish swim.

"Work, fish, work," he thought.

A soft wind was blowing.

"I will find my way home. **Cuba** is a long island."

Chapter 21
The Death of the Marlin

He saw the fish. The fish swam around three times. The fish was very big.

"Really? Is the fish really that big?" he said.

The old man saw the fish. The fish had a big body. The fish swam to the top of the water. The fish was thirty meters away. He saw the fish's tail come up. The tail was purple. He could see the fish. The fish had a big body.

The old man could see the fish's eye. Two gray fish were with the big fish. Sometimes they were close to the big fish. Sometimes they were far from the big fish. The gray fish were three feet long.

The old man was sweating. He pulled in more line when the fish came close to him.

"I will push this harpoon into the fish," he thought.

"Be strong, old man," he said.

The fish turned around again. The fish's back was out of the water. But the fish was too far from the boat. When the fish turned again, it was higher. The old man knew it was time to catch the fish. His harpoon was ready.

The fish was swimming in a circle. The fish moved its great

tail. The old man pulled the fishing line. The fish turned on its side for a little bit.

"I made the fish turn over," the old man said. "I made him turn over."

The old man felt sick in the head. He held onto the fish.

"Pull, hands! Come on, legs! I will pull the fish into the boat."

But the fish swam away.

"Fish, you are going to die," the old man said. "Do you have to kill me too?"

His mouth was too dry to speak. He could not get water.

"I need the fish to swim close to the boat," he thought.

The fish swam away again.

"You are killing me," the old man thought. "But you have a right to do that. You are a great fish. I have never seen a fish like you. Come and kill me. I don't care."

"I am confused," he thought. "I need to have a clear mind."

"Clear up!" he said.

The fish swam around again. "I do not know what to do," the old man thought. "But I will try again."

The old man tried. He felt sick in the head. Nothing changed.

"I will try again," he said.

He tried again. He couldn't catch the fish.

The old man pulled the line with all his strength. He felt pain, but he still pulled it. The fish came to the boat. Then the fish swam past the boat.

The old man dropped the fishing line. He stepped on the line. He lifted up his harpoon. He pushed his harpoon into the fish.

The fish jumped up. Then it fell into the water again.

The old man felt sick in the head. The fish was turned over. Blood came from the fish's heart. The blood looked like a cloud.

Chapter 22
Tying the Marlin to the Boat

The old man looked at the fish. He put his head in his hands.

"Stay strong," he said to himself. "I am tired. But now I have the fish. I have to work."

"I have to prepare the rope and tie the fish to the boat," he thought. "If I put the fish in the boat, the boat will break. I will tie the fish to the boat and go home."

He started to pull the fish in.

"I want to see and touch the fish," he thought. "When I pushed on the harpoon, I felt his heart. I will pull in the fish and tie it to the boat."

"Get to work, old man," he said.

He drank some water.

"I have so much work to do."

The old man looked at the sky. He looked at the sun. It was afternoon. The wind from the east was blowing.

"Come on, fish," he said.

But the fish did not come. The old man pulled the boat to the fish.

The old man was close to the fish. He saw the fish's head. The fish's head was huge. He untied the rope on the harpoon.

The old man tied the fish's head to the boat. He tied the fish's tail to the boat. The fish was a silver color.

"That was the only way to kill him," the old man said.
The old man felt better after he drank water. His head was clear.
"The fish is over 700 kilograms," he thought. "How much will the fish cost per kilo?"
"I need a pencil," he said. "My head is not that clear."

He tied the fish tightly. The fish was so big. It was like a big boat. He cut a piece of line. He tied up the fish's mouth. He set up the sail on the boat. He sailed southwest.

He did not need a compass. He knew how to sail southwest.
"I need food and water," he thought.
He caught some yellow seaweed. He shook the yellow seaweed. Small shrimps were inside the seaweed. The small shrimps fell onto the boat. There were more than ten shrimps. He ate them all. The shrimps were small, but they tasted good.

The old man still had some water. He drank a little water after he ate. The boat was sailing. He could see the fish. He looked at his hands. It was not a dream. He thought that he was dreaming before. When the fish came out of the water, he thought he was dreaming. But now he knew. It was not a dream.

Now he knew that everything was true. The fish was there with him. The old man felt pain in his hands.

"The hands will get better," he thought. "Salt water will help. Salt water is good for my hands. I have to keep my head clear."

Then, the old man did not know what to do.
"Is the fish pulling me? Am I pulling the fish?"
"Maybe the fish is pulling me."

Chapter 23
The Mako Shark

They sailed well. The old man put his hands in the salt water. Clouds were in the sky. He kept looking at the fish. One hour later, a shark came up.

The shark came up from the deep sea. The shark smelled the blood. It jumped up from the water. Then it followed the boat.

Sometimes the shark could not smell the fish. The shark smelled the fish again. The shark swam fast. It was a very big **Mako** shark. The shark was beautiful. But the shark's mouth was not beautiful. The **Mako** shark looked like a swordfish. The shark swam fast in the water. The shark had a lot of teeth. The teeth were long like fingers. The teeth looked like claws. Sharks can eat many fish. Sharks are strong. The shark sped up and followed the boat. The shark's fin came out of the water.

The old man saw the shark coming. The shark was not scared. He prepared the harpoon. He watched the shark come up. His head felt good. He looked at the fish.
He watched the shark come close.
"I wish this was a dream," he thought.

The shark came closer. The old man saw the shark's

mouth open wide. He saw the shark's eyes and teeth. The shark ate the fish. The old man pushed the harpoon into the shark's head. The harpoon hit the shark's brain.

The shark turned over. The old man saw that the shark's eyes were dying. The old man knew that the shark was dead. The shark's tail hit the water. The shark's body came up out of the water. Then it went down into the water.

"The shark took about twenty kilograms from my fish," he said out loud.
"The shark took my harpoon and rope too," he thought.
He did not like to look at the fish anymore.
"I killed the shark," he thought. "He was the biggest **Mako** shark."

"I wish it was a dream," he thought. "I wish I was in bed. I am sad that I killed the fish. The bad time is coming. I do not have the harpoon. Sharks are strong and smart. But I was smarter."
"Don't think, old man," he said out loud. "Keep sailing."

"But I must think," he thought. "All I can do is think. I hit the shark in the brain. What would the great **DiMaggio** think? My hands were in pain. He has pain in his feet. I don't know which one hurts more."

"Think about something joyful," he said. "I'm getting closer to home. The boat became twenty kilograms lighter."

"Yes, there is," he said out loud. "I have a knife. I am an old man, but I have the knife."

The breeze was fresh. The old man kept sailing. He checked on the front part of the fish. He had hope.

"It is foolish to have no hope," he thought. "It is wrong to have no hope. Maybe it was wrong to kill the fish. Do not think about that. I was born to be a fisherman. I was just doing my job."

He liked to think about himself. There was nothing to do. There was nothing to read. He did not have a radio. He thought for a long time.

"You didn't kill the fish to sell it," he thought. "You have pride. That's why you killed the fish. You are a fisherman."

"You think too much," he said out loud.

"But you liked killing the Mako shark," he thought.

"I killed the shark to save myself," the old man said out loud. "I did well."

"Everything kills something in some way," he thought.

He leaned against the boat. He took a piece of the fish. He chewed the flesh. It tasted very good. He wanted to sell the fish at the market. But a very hard time was coming.

Chapter 24
The Two Sharks

The wind blew. The old man looked ahead. He could not see other boats. There was only the flying fish.

He sailed for two hours. Sometimes he ate some of the marlin. He tried to rest. He saw another shark.

"Ay," he said out loud.

"Shark," he said out loud. He saw the second shark. These sharks were called **shovel-nosed** sharks. The sharks smelled the fish. They swam as fast as they could.

He held the knife tightly. He watched the sharks come up. He saw their heads and their fins. The sharks hated everything. The sharks smelled bad. The sharks wanted to eat everything.

"Ay," the old man said. "Come on sharks."

They came. One shark went under the boat. The old man felt the boat shake. The other shark came and bit the fish. The old man put his knife into the shark's head. The old man put his knife into the shark's eyes. The shark went down into the water.

The boat was shaking. The other shark bit the fish. The other shark came out from under the boat. The old man hit the shark with the knife. The knife didn't go in deep. Then the shark came up again. The old man hit the middle of the shark's head. He hit the same spot again. But the shark was not dead.

"No?" the old man said.
He hit the shark's head again. A bone broke. The shark was dead. The shark fell into the deep water.
"Go on. Go see your friend," he said.
The old man cleaned off his knife.

Chapter 25
The Broken Knife

"The shark ate many parts of the fish," he said out loud. "I wish it were a dream. I wish I had never caught this fish."
He stopped to speak. He did not want to look at the fish.
"I shouldn't have gone out so far," he said. "I'm sorry, fish."
"Sharks will come again," he said. "I'll prepare for the next time."

"I wish I had a stone for the knife," the old man said.

"You needed so many things," he thought. "But you did not bring them, old man. Now is not the time to think."

"You think too much," he said. "I'm tired of it."

The boat sailed. The old man put his hands in the water. The boat was much lighter. He did not want to think about the fish. The smell went out in the water. More sharks could smell the fish.

"It was a big fish," he thought. "Don't think of that. Just rest and prepare your hands."

His hand was not bleeding.

"What can I think about?" he thought. "Nothing. I will not think. I will wait for sharks to come."

"I really wish it were a dream."

The next shark came to the boat. The shark opened its mouth wide. The shark was like a pig with a big mouth. The old man pushed his knife into the shark. But the knife broke.

The old man sailed the boat again. The shark was dead. The shark went down into the water. The shark looked smaller and smaller.

"I have the gaff," he said. "But it will not help me."

"I lost," he thought. "I am too old to hit sharks with a club."

He put his hands in the water. It was late in the afternoon.

He could not see the land. He wanted to see the land.

"You're tired," he said. "You're tired inside."

It was evening. The old man saw brown fins coming. They came straight to the boat.

He stopped the boat. He held the club with his right hand. He saw two sharks come.

"I have to hit the shark's head or his nose," he thought.

The two sharks came close to the boat. One shark opened his mouth.

The old man raised his club. He hit the shark on the head. He hit the shark's nose.

The other shark went in. Then it came out. It came in again. The old man hit the shark with his club. He hit the shark's head. The shark looked at him. The shark bit the fish one more time. The old man hit him with the club again. The shark moved away.

"Come on, Shark," the old man said. "Come in again."

The shark swam up fast. The old man hit the shark. He hit the shark from up high. The old man felt the shark's bone. He hit the shark again. The shark moved away.

The old man waited for the sharks to come. But the sharks did not come.

"I could not kill them," he thought. "But I have hurt them. They must feel bad right now."

Chapter 26
Half of the Fish

He did not want to look at the fish. Half of the fish was gone. The sun went down.

"It will be dark soon," he said. "I will see the lights of Havana."

"I will arrive soon," he thought. "I hope no one was worried. The boy will be worried. Older fishermen will be worried too. I live in a good town."

He could not talk to the fish. The fish was torn up.
"Half fish," he said. "I am sorry I went too far out. But we killed many sharks. How many sharks did you kill?"

"What will you do if the sharks come in the night? What can you do?" he thought.
"Fight them," he said. "I will fight them until I die."

It was night. There was no light. There was only the wind. The old man felt like he was dead. He put his hands together. He leaned back. He felt pain. He was not dead. His pain told him. He was alive.

"I promised to pray," he thought. "But I am too tired to pray."
He lay in the boat. He looked for the lights.

"I have half of the fish," he thought. "I wish I could bring the fish home. I think I have some luck."

"I want to buy some luck," he said.
"What can I buy luck with?" he asked himself. "Can I buy luck with a lost harpoon? Can I buy it with a broken knife?"
"Maybe you can," he said.
"I must not think silly things," he thought. "I wish I could see the lights."
He tried to sit down.

Chapter 27
The Last Fight

He saw the lights of the city. The lights were dim. But he could see the lights from his place on the ocean. He sailed toward the lights.

"Now it's over," he thought. "The sharks will come. I don't have a harpoon. I don't have a knife. How do I fight the sharks?"

The old man's body was sick.

"I hope I don't have to fight sharks again," he thought.

The sharks came at midnight. The old man fought the sharks. The sharks came in a group. The sharks shook the boat. The old man could feel the sharks and hear them. He hit the sharks. A shark took his club.

The sharks came together. They took off the pieces of the fish. They came back for more.

One last shark came to the fish. The shark ate the fish. Now, there was nothing for the sharks to eat. The fish was gone.

The old man could hardly breathe. He felt something in his mouth. It was blood. The old man spit it out.
"Eat that, sharks," he said.

The old man knew he had lost. He sailed the boat again.

The boat was lighter. The old man did not think. He sailed the boat to his home port. The sharks came again in the night. The old man did not care. He only cared about sailing.

"The boat is good," he thought. "The boat is not broken."
He could see the lights of the beach. He knew where he was.

"Sometimes the wind is our friend," he thought. "The sea is our friend. The sea is also our enemy. My bed is my friend. Going to bed is a good thing."

He sailed into the little harbor. The lights of the Terrace were out. He knew everyone was in bed. It was quiet in the harbor. He tied his boat to a rock.

He pulled the mast. He carried the mast on his shoulder. He climbed toward home. He was so tired. He stopped. He looked back at the fish. Only the bones of the fish were left.

He started to climb again. He fell down. He was on the ground with the mast. He tried to get up.

It was too difficult. He sat there and watched the road.

He stood up and picked the mast up. He started to walk. He sat down five times on the way home. He arrived at his tiny house. He leaned the mast on the wall.

He found a water bottle and drank water. Then he lay down on the bed. He went to sleep.

Chapter 28
At Home

The boy came to the old man's house in the morning. The old man was breathing. He was asleep. The boy saw the old man's hands. He started to cry. He went out to buy coffee for the old man. He kept crying while he was going.

Many fishermen were looking at the old man's boat. The fish was eaten by the sharks. Only fish bones were there.
"How is he?" one of the fishermen asked the boy.
"Sleeping," the boy said.
The boy was still crying.
"Let him sleep more."

The boy went into the Terrace. He asked for a can of coffee.
"I want hot coffee. Put in milk and sugar, please."
"Do you want anything else?"
"No, thank you."
"Do you want a drink for you?"
"No," the boy said. "I'll be back."
"Tell Santiago that I am sorry."
"Thanks," the boy said.

The boy came back to the old man's house. The old man was still asleep. The boy sat by him until he woke up. The boy waited a long time. Finally, the old man woke up.

"Rest here," the boy said. "Drink this."

The old man took the coffee and drank it.

"I lost, **Manolin**," he said. "I lost."

"No, you didn't. You got the fish."

"I lost after I caught the fish."

"Did they look for me?" the old man asked.

"Yes. They looked for you with airplanes."

"The ocean is very big," the old man said. "I missed you. What did you catch?"

"I caught one on the first day. I caught one on the second day. I caught two on the third day," the boy said.

"Very good."

"Now we will fish together."

"No. I am not lucky. I am not lucky anymore."

"I will bring luck," the boy said.

"I caught two fish yesterday. I have to learn more. We will fish together."

"We need a good knife. My knife broke," the old man said.

"I'll get another knife," the boy said. "I will get everything ready. Let your hands rest, old man."

"I will care for my hands."

"Lie down, old man. I will bring you your clean shirt. I will bring you food."

"Bring me the newspapers," the old man said.

"You must take a good rest. Did you have a hard time?"

"It was a very hard time," the old man said.

"I'll bring the food and newspapers," the boy said. "Rest well, old man."

The boy went out the door. He was crying again. People were having a party at the Terrace. It was afternoon. They looked down and saw the big bones of the fish near the boat. The old man was still sleeping in his house. The boy was sitting by him. The old man was dreaming about the lions.

Level 3은 여전히 쉬운 단어를 사용하지만
원문을 이해하는데 필요한 핵심 정보들이 추가 되었어요.

Level 2를 읽고 여기까지 오셨다면 어렵지 않게 읽을 수 있습니다.

원문에 쓰인 스페인어는 굵게 표시했습니다.

THE ORIGINAL TEXT

"Be patient, hand," he said. "I do this for you." I wish I could feed the fish, he thought. He is my brother. But I must kill him and keep strong to do it. Slowly and conscientiously he ate all of the wedge-shaped strips of fish. He straightened up, wiping his hand on his trousers.

LEVEL 3

"Be patient, hand," he said. "I am doing this for you." "I wish I could feed the fish," he thought. "The fish is my brother. But I must kill the fish."
He slowly ate all of the pieces of fish. He stood up straight and wiped his hand on his pants.

The Old Man and the Sea

LEVEL 3

Chapter 1
The Old Man and the Boy

He was an old man who fished alone in the sea. He had been empty-handed for eighty-four days. In the first forty days, a boy had been with him. But after forty days, the boy's parents had told him that the old man was completely unlucky and ordered their son to join another boat.

The boy was sad to see the old man come back with an empty boat every day. The boy always went down to help him carry fishing tools, such as lines, a gaff, a harpoon, and a sail. The sail was old and folded. It looked like the flag of a loser.

The old man was thin and lean. He had deep wrinkles on the back of his neck. The brown spots caused by the sun's reflection were on his cheeks. His hands had deep scars from handling fish on the cords. These scars were old.

Everything about him was old except his eyes. His eyes were the same color as the sea.

"Santiago," the boy said to him as they went up the bank. "I could go with you again. We've made some money."

The old man had taught the boy how to fish.

"No," the old man said. "You're with a lucky boat. Stay with them."

"But remember we caught some big fish after 87 days."

"I remember," the old man said. "I know you did not leave me because you didn't trust me."

"It was Papa who made me leave. I must obey him."

"I know," the old man said. "It is normal."

"Can I offer you a beer on the Terrace, and then we'll take the stuff home."

"Why not?" the old man said. "Between fishermen."

They sat on the Terrace, and many of the fishermen made fun of the old man. Other fishermen looked at him and were sad. But they did not show it.

Chapter 2
Friendship

The successful fishermen of that day had already come back. They had cleaned their marlin. They carried the marlin, laid across two boards, to the fish house. They waited for the ice truck to carry them to the market in Havana.

Those who had caught sharks had taken them to the shark factory on the other side of a small bay. The sharks were lifted by a pulley. The fishermen cut out the livers, fins, and flesh from the sharks.

When the wind was in the east, a smell came from the shark factory. But today there was not a strong smell because the wind blew back to the north. It was pleasant and sunny on the Terrace.

"Santiago," the boy said.
"Yes," the old man said. He was thinking while holding his glass.
"Can I go out to get sardines for you for tomorrow?"
"No. Go and play baseball."
"I would like to go. If I can't go with you, I would like to help you in some way."
"You bought me a beer," the old man said.

"How old was I when you first took me in a boat?"

"You were five, and you almost died when I caught a tough fish. Do you remember?"

"I remember the tail slapping and the seat breaking and the clubbing sound. I remember you pushing me into the front of the boat for safety. I felt the whole boat move up and down."

"Can you really remember that? Or did I just tell it to you?"

"I remember everything from when we first went together." The old man looked at him with loving eyes.

"If you were my boy, I'd take you out," he said. "But you are your parent's son."

"May I get the sardines? I know where I can get four baits too. I have mine left from today. I put them in salt in the box. Let me get four fresh ones."

"One is okay," the old man said. His hope and his confidence had never gone.

"Two," the boy said.

"Two," the old man agreed. "You didn't steal them?"

"I would," the boy said. "But I bought these."

"Thank you," the old man said. He knew he had achieved humility, but he was not embarrassed.

"Tomorrow is going to be a good day with this current," he said.

"Where are you going?" the boy asked.

"Far out, to come in when the wind shifts. I want to be out before sunrise."

"I'll try to get him to fish far out," the boy said. "Then if you catch big fish, we can come to help you."

"He does not like to fish too far out."

"But I will see something that he cannot see and get him to come out after dolphinfish," the boy said.

"Are his eyes that bad?"

"He is almost blind."

"It is strange," the old man said. "He never went turtle-ing. Turtle-ing strains the eyes."

"But you went turtle-ing for years and your eyes are good."

"I am a strange old man."

"But are you strong enough to catch a huge fish?"

"I think so. And there are many tricks."

"Let us take the stuff home," the boy said. "So I can get the cast net and catch the sardines."

They picked up the stuff from the boat. The old man carried the mast and the boy carried the wooden box with the lines, the gaff, and the harpoon. The box with the baits and the club was left on the boat. No one would steal from the old man, but it was better to take the mast and the wooden box home.

Chapter 3
The Shack

They walked up the road together to the old man's cottage and went in through the open door. The old man leaned the mast against the wall and the boy put the box and the other things beside it. The mast was almost as long as the one room of the cottage.

The cottage was made of the tough bark of the royal palm which is called '***guano***', and in it there was a bed, a table, one chair and a place to cook on the dirt floor. On the brown wall, there was a picture in color of the Sacred Heart of Jesus and another of the Virgin of Cobre. These belonged to his wife. Once there was a photo of his wife on the wall, but he took it off. The old man's clean shirt was on the shelf in the corner.

"What do you have to eat?" the boy asked.

"A pot of yellow rice with fish. Do you want some?"

"No, I will eat at home. Do you want me to make the fire?"

"No. I will make it later on, or I may eat the rice cold."

"May I take the cast net?"

"Of course."

There was no cast net and no pot of yellow rice and fish. But they went through this fiction every day.

"Eighty-five is a lucky number," the old man said. "How would you like to see me catch a fish that's over a thousand pounds?"

"I'll get the cast net and go catch sardines. Will you sit in the doorway?"

"Yes, I have yesterday's newspaper and I will read about baseball."

The boy did not know whether yesterday's paper was a made-up story too. But the old man brought it out from under the bed.

"Perico gave it to me at the bar," he explained.

"I'll be back when I have the sardines. I'll keep yours and mine together on ice and we can use them together in the morning. When I come back, you can tell me about the baseball game."

"The New York Yankees cannot lose."

"But I fear the Cleveland Indians."

"Have faith in the New York Yankees, my son. Think of the great DiMaggio."

"I am afraid of both the Detroit Tigers and the Cleveland Indians."

"Be careful or you will even be afraid of the Chicago White Sox."

"You read about it and tell me when I come back."

"Do you think we should buy a lottery ticket with an eighty-five? Tomorrow is the eighty-fifth day."

"We can do that," the boy said. "But what about the eighty-seven of your great record?"

"It could not happen twice. Do you think you can find an eighty-five?"

"I can order one."

"One sheet. That's two dollars and a half."

"Keep warm old man," the boy said. "Remember we are in September."

"This is the month when the great fish come," the old man said. "Anyone can be a fisherman in May."

"I will go get the sardines now," the boy said.

When the boy came back, the old man was asleep in the chair, and the sun had set. The boy took the old army blanket off the bed and spread it over the old man's shoulders. The old man's shoulders and neck were still strong, though they were very old. His old skin did not show so much because his head had fallen forward. His shirt had been repaired so many times. The old man's head was very old. When his eyes were closed, there was no life in his face.

The newspaper was on his lap, and he was not wearing shoes.

Chapter 4
The Baseball Game

The boy left him there, and when he came back, the old man was still sleeping.

"Wake up old man," the boy said and he put his hand on the old man's knees.

The old man opened his eyes, then he smiled.

"What have you got?" the old man asked.

"I have supper for us," said the boy. "We are going to have supper."

"I'm not very hungry."

"Come on and eat. You can't go fishing without eating anything."

"I have done that many times," the old man said.

The old man was getting up and taking the newspaper and folding it. "What are we eating?"

"Black beans and rice, fried bananas, and some stew," the boy answered.

The boy brought them boxes of food from the Terrace. Two sets of knives, forks, and spoons were in his pocket.

"Who gave this to you?"

"Martin. The owner of the Terrace."

"I should thank him."

"I thanked him already," the boy said. "You don't need to thank him."

"I will give him the belly meat of a big fish," the old man said.

"He also gave us two beers."

"I like the beer in cans best."

"I know, but this is in bottles. I take back the bottles."

"That's very kind of you," the old man said.

"Should we eat?"

"I asked you to eat before," the boy told him gently. "I didn't want to open the boxes until you were ready to eat."

"I'm ready now," the old man said. "I only needed time to wash."

"Where did he wash?" the boy thought. "The village water supply was two streets down the road. I should prepare water for him. I should get him another shirt and a jacket for the winter."

"Your stew is excellent," the old man said.

"Tell me about the baseball game," the boy asked him.

"The best team in the American League is the Yankees," the old man said happily.

"They lost today," the boy told him.

"That means nothing. The great DiMaggio is doing well again."

"They have other men on the Yankees team."

"Sure. But the great DiMaggio makes a difference," the old man said. "In the other league, Philadelphia I think, there is Dick Sisler."

"You're right, Dick Sisler hits the longest ball I have ever seen."

"Do you remember when he used to come to the Terrace?"

"I wanted to take him fishing but I was too shy to ask him."

"I asked you to ask him but you were shy too."

"I know. It was a great mistake. He might have gone with us," the boy said.

"I would like to take the great DiMaggio fishing," the old man said. "People say his father was a fisherman. Maybe he was as poor as we are."

"The great Sisler's father was never poor. He was already a baseball player at my age."

"When I was your age, I went to Africa on a ship with a four-sided sail and I saw lions on the beaches."

"I know. You told me."

"Should we talk about Africa or about baseball?"

"Baseball, I think," the boy said. "Tell me about the great John J. McGraw."

"He used to come to the Terrace sometimes. But he was rough and difficult when he drank beer. His mind was on horse racing as well as baseball. He always carried a paper with lists of horses in his pocket."

"He was a great manager," the boy said. "My father thinks he was the greatest."

"That's because he came here the most times," the old man said.

"Who is the greatest manager, really, Luque or Mike Gonzalez?" the boy asked.

"I think they are equal."

"And the best fisherman is you."

"No. I know other fishermen who are better than me."

"No way," the boy said. "There are many good fishermen, but you are the best."

"Thank you. You make me happy."

"I hope I will not meet a fish that is too big for me."

"If you are still strong, there is no fish like that."

"I may not be as strong as I think," the old man said. "But I don't give up easily."

"You have to go to bed now so that you will be fresh in the morning."

"Good night then. I will wake you in the morning."

"You're my alarm clock," the boy said.

"Age is my alarm clock," the old man said. "Why do old men wake so early?"

"I don't know," the boy said.

"I'll wake you up in time."

"I do not like it when he wakes me up."

"I understand."

"Sleep well, old man."

"Sleep well."

Chapter 5
Going Fishing

The boy went out. They had eaten their food at the table in the dark. The old man removed his pants in the dark and went to bed. He rolled his pants up to make a pillow. He lay on the bed with a blanket around him.

He fell asleep quickly and he dreamed of when he was a boy in Africa. He saw the long golden beaches, the white beaches, and the big brown mountains. He dreamed that he was on that coast every night. He heard the sound of waves and saw the boats sailing. He smelled the smell of tar and old rope. He smelled the smell of Africa in the morning breeze.

Usually, when he smelled this breeze, he woke up, got dressed, and went to wake up the boy. But tonight the smell of Africa came too early. He kept dreaming. He saw the white mountains of the Canary Islands and the different ports.

He no longer dreamed of storms, women, great fish, fighting, or his wife. He only dreamed of places and of the lions on the beach. The lions played like young cats and he loved them like he loved the boy. He woke up, and he looked out the open door at the moon. He put on his pants and went to wake up the boy.

He was shaking in the cold.

He went to the boy's house. The house was unlocked. He opened the door and walked in quietly. The boy was asleep on a small bed in the first room. The old man could see him in the moonlight. He touched the boy's foot gently until the boy woke up. The boy woke up and looked at him. The old man greeted him and the boy took his pants from the chair. The boy sat on the bed and put on his pants. The old man went out the door and the boy came after him. The boy was sleepy.

The old man put his arm across the boy's shoulders and said, "I am sorry."

"No, it is what a man must do," the boy said.

They walked down the road to the old man's cottage. On the road, fishermen were moving, carrying their masts. They reached the old man's cottage. The boy took the rolls of line, the harpoon, and the gaff. The old man carried the mast on his shoulder.

"Do you want coffee?" the boy asked.

"We'll put the things in the boat and then get some."

They drank coffee from milk cans at the local coffee shop.

"How did you sleep, old man?" the boy asked. He was waking up now.

"Very well, Manolin," the old man said. "I feel confident today."

"So do I," the boy said. "Now I have to get sardines for

you and me and your fresh baits."

"Thank you. You carried things for me when you were five years old," the old man said.

"I'll be right back," the boy said. "Have another coffee."

He walked to the ice house where the baits were. The old man drank his coffee slowly. It was the only thing he would have all day. For a long time now, eating was not interesting to him, and he never brought lunch. He had a bottle of water in the front of the boat.

The boy came back with the sardines and the two baits. They went down the path to the boat. They felt the sand under their feet. They pushed the boat into the water.

"Good luck, old man."

"Good luck," the old man said.

He fitted the oars onto the oarlock. He began to row out of the harbor in the dark. There were other boats from the other harbors going out to sea. The old man heard the push of their oars even though he could not see them.

Chapter 6
Bait

Sometimes someone in a boat would say something. But most of the boats were silent except for the push of the oars. They sailed out of the harbor. They moved to parts of the ocean where they hoped to find fish. The old man decided to go far out. He left the land behind and rowed out into the ocean.

He saw the light of the Gulf weed in the water as he rowed over a part of the ocean called "the great well." The fishermen called this part "the great well" because there was a big hole there. The hole was more than 1 kilometer deep. The movement of the current brought all sorts of fish there. There were shrimps, baitfish, and squid. At night, they came close to the surface.

In the dark, the old man could feel the morning coming. He rowed away. He heard the sound of flying fish jumping out of the water. Their hard wings made sounds as they flew away. The flying fish were his friends on the ocean, and he liked them.

He felt sorry for the birds, especially small birds, called sea swallows. They were always looking but rarely finding fish. He thought that the birds have a harder life than us, except for the big birds.

Why were these birds weak and small? For small birds, the sea was cruel. The sea is kind and very beautiful. But she can also be so cruel.

The old man always thought of the sea as "**la mar**", which is in the female form in Spanish. Sometimes people say bad things about the sea. But they always speak as if the sea were a woman. Some of the younger fishermen made a lot of money from catching sharks. They bought motorboats. They spoke of the sea as "**el mar**", which is in the male form. But the old man always thought of the sea in the female form. If the sea did wild or bad things it was because the sea could not help people.

He was rowing steadily and it was no effort for him. He continued to go at the same speed. The surface of the ocean was flat. He was letting the current do some of the work. He rowed along the current. Daylight was coming. He saw that he was further out than he wanted to be.

"I fished for a week at deep wells and I didn't catch anything," he thought. "Today I'll go where the schools of tuna are. Maybe there will be a big fish there."

Before it was light, he had his baits out. He let the boat drift away with the current. One bait was down 72 meters. The second one was down 135 meters. The third one and fourth one were down 180 and 225 meters. Each bait hung head-down with the hook. All the points of the hook were covered with fresh sardines. Each sardine was hooked through both eyes. A big fish could feel every part of the hook, it would be sweet smelling and good tasting.

The boy had given him two fresh, small tunas. The tunas hung on the two deepest fishing lines. The old man hung a blue runner fish and yellow jack fish on the other lines. They were used before, but they were still in good condition. There were excellent sardines that had a good smell. Each line was as thick as a big pencil. There was a green float stick on the fishing lines. If a fish came and pulled on the bait, the stick would go down. Each line had 72 meters of coils. They could connect to the other extra coils.

Now the old man watched the three sticks over the side of the boat. He rowed carefully to keep the fishing lines straight up and down. He kept them at their proper depths. It would soon be light. The sun would soon come up. The sun rose up above the sea and the old man could see the other boats. The other boats were spread out across the current. Then the sun was brighter. The glare came on the water. When the sun rose, the sea sent the light back at his eyes. His eyes hurt badly. He rowed without looking into the light.

He looked down into the water. He watched the lines that went straight down into the darkness. He kept the lines straighter than anyone did. The lines always went down to where he wanted them to be. Other fishermen let the lines drift with the current. The depth of those lines was not accurate.

But he thought, "I keep the lines in the right place. Only I have no luck anymore. But who knows? Maybe today is the day. Every day is a new day."

Chapter 7
A Man-Of-War Bird

The sun had come up two hours ago. It did not hurt his eyes to look into the east. There were only three boats in sight. They showed very low and close to the shore.

He thought, "All my life, the early morning sun has hurt my eyes. Yet they are still good. I can look straight into the evening sunset, but the morning sunlight is painful to look at."

Just then, he saw a man-of-war bird flying in a circle with his long black wings. The bird dropped down and flew in a circle again.

"He's got something," the old man said aloud. "He's not just looking."

He rowed slowly toward the bird. He did not hurry, and he kept his lines straight up and down. He was still fishing the right way.

The bird went higher in the air and flew in a circle again. Then the bird dipped down suddenly, and the old man saw flying fish. The flying fish jumped out of the water and flew over it.

"Dolphin," the old man said aloud. "Big dolphin."

He put his oars inside the boat. He brought a small fishing line from the front of the boat. The line had a wire leader and a hook. The hook was medium-sized. He put a sardine on the hook. He let it go over the side and then tied it tightly to the boat. He prepared another fishing line. He went back to rowing and to watching the black bird.

The bird dropped down again. The bird flapped its wings and followed the flying fish. The old man could see the school of dolphins. They followed the flying fish. They swam under the flying fish.

He thought, "It is a big school of dolphins. They're going to catch the flying fish. The bird has no chance to get the flying fish. The flying fish are too big for the bird."

He watched the flying fish jump out of the water again and again. He also watched the bird moving and not catching anything.

"The school of dolphins went away from me," he thought. "They are moving too fast. They are going out far. But maybe I will catch some extra fish behind them. Maybe my big fish is around them. My big fish is somewhere out there."

The clouds rose up over the land like mountains. The coast was like a long green line with blue and gray hills. The water was a dark blue color now. It was almost purple. He saw the red plankton in the dark water. Now the light shining down from the sun was strange. He checked the fishing lines. He was happy to see so much plankton because it meant that fish were there.

The sun was shining. It was shining a strange light onto the water. The sun was higher, and the clouds looked like mountains. This meant the weather was good. But the bird was almost out of sight. There was nothing to see on the surface of the water. Some yellow seaweed and a large purple jellyfish were there. The jellyfish floated like a bubble. The long, purple arms of the jellyfish stretched out far behind it.

"This is bad water," the old man said. "You are sneaky."

He looked down into the water while he rowed softly. He saw the tiny fish that were the same color as the jellyfish. The tiny fish swam between the jellyfish. They were safe from the jellyfish's poison. But humans could not handle the poison. Sometimes these jellyfish would stick to a line and hurt the old man's hands.

The jellyfish made beautiful bubbles with rainbow colors. But they were very tricky. The old man loved to see the big sea turtles eating the jellyfish. When the turtles saw the jellyfish, they approached them from the front. Then the turtles closed their eyes and ate them all. The old man loved to see the turtles eat them. He also loved to walk over them on the beach after a storm.

He loved green turtles and hawk-bill turtles with their style and speed. They were valued at a high price. But he joked with the huge loggerhead turtles. Sometimes he liked the huge loggerhead turtles. Sometimes he didn't like them.

He didn't have any ideas about turtles. He had hunted turtles for many years. Some of the turtles were as long as a boat and weighed one ton. He was sorry for them all. A turtle's heart will beat for hours after death, even if the turtle has been cut up. Most people don't care about turtles.

The old man thought, "My feet, hands, and heart are like theirs."

He ate some white turtle eggs to give himself strength so he could catch a really big fish.

He also drank a cup of shark liver oil. Most fishermen hated the taste. But it was good for colds and good for the eyes.

Chapter 8
Albacore

Now the old man looked up and saw the bird flying in a circle again.

"The bird found fish," he said aloud.

There was no flying fish. There was no bait fish. But the old man watched the sea. At that moment, a small tuna jumped out of the water and dropped back down head first. Another tuna jumped up and another jumped up. Then the tuna jumped from all directions. They were circling and following the bait fish.

He thought, "If they are not too fast, I will sail into this group of fish."

He watched the school of tuna turning the water white and the bird trying to catch the fish.

"The bird is a great help," the old man said.

Just then the fishing line moved. The line was stretched tightly under his foot. He dropped his oars. He started to pull up the fishing line. He felt the weight of the fish. He pulled up the line. It was a small tuna. He could see that the fish had a blue back and gold sides. He swung the fish over the side and into the boat. The tuna lay in the back of the boat. The tuna was small. The tuna had a bullet shape. The tuna hit the boat with the quick-moving tail. The old man was kind. He hit the tuna on the head to make it faint, and he kicked it.

"This is Albacore," he said out loud. "It will be good for bait. It will weigh ten pounds."

He did not know when he started talking to himself. A long time ago, he sang songs alone at night in the fishing boats.

He may have started talking out loud when the boy left. But he did not remember. Even when they were fishing together, they spoke only when they had to. This is normal for people who went fishing.

"If the others heard me talking out loud to myself, they would think that I am crazy," he said. "But since I am not crazy, I do not care. And the rich men have radios. They can listen to the news and hear the baseball updates on the boat."

"Now is not the time to think of baseball," he thought. "Now is the time to think of one thing. That is fishing. Maybe a big fish is around here. I picked up only one small tuna. The fish that I saw today moved fast and to the northeast. Is it a special time of day? Or is it because of the weather? I do not know."

Now he could not see the green of the shore. He could

only see the tops of the hills. The hills looked like they were covered in snow. The clouds looked like high, snowy mountains. The sea was very dark, and the light made prisms in the water. There was no plankton now because the sun was high. The old man only saw the deep prisms in the blue. His fishing lines went into the water.

Chapter 9
Encounter

The tunas were gone. The fishermen called all fish of that kind 'tuna'. They only used their correct names when they were selling or trading for baits. Now the sun was hot. The old man felt it on the back of his neck and felt the sweat drip down his back.

"I could just drift," the old man thought. "I could get some sleep, but I should catch a big fish."

Just then, he saw the green stick go down suddenly.

"Yes," he said. "Yes."

He put his oars inside the boat quietly. He reached out for the fishing line. He held it softly between his thumb and finger. He did not feel any weight or pressure. A little later he felt something pulling the line. He knew what it was. It was a marlin eating the sardines that covered the hook.

The old man held the line carefully and softly. Then he

untied the line from the stick with his left hand.

"This fish must be huge this time," he thought. "Eat the baits, fish. Eat them. Please eat them. They are so fresh. And you are down there, one hundred eighty-two meters deep in the cold water."

He felt the light pulling and then harder pulling. Then there was nothing.

"Come on," the old man said aloud. "Turn around again. Just smell them. Aren't they wonderful? Eat up, and then there is tuna for you. Don't be shy, fish. Eat them."

He waited, holding the fishing line between his thumb and his finger. He watched it and other lines at the same time. Then he felt the soft pulling again.

"The fish will take it," the old man said out loud. "God, please help the fish to take the bait."

But the fish did not take it. The fish was gone and the old man felt nothing.

"It could not have gone. The fish is turning back. Maybe the fish was hooked before and it remembers that time," he said.

Then he felt the gentle touch on the line, and he was happy.

"The fish just turned," he said. "The fish will take it."

He was happy to feel the gentle pulling. But then he felt something hard and so heavy. It was the weight of the fish. He let the line slip down deeper. The fishing line unrolled and used the extra fishing lines. The fishing line went down. It slipped lightly through the old man's fingers. He still felt the weight of the big fish.

"What a fish," he said. "The fish has the bait in the side of its mouth."

"Then the fish will swallow the bait," he thought.

He did not say that, because he knew that if he said something good, it might not happen. He knew what a huge fish this was. He thought of it moving away with the tuna in its mouth. At that moment, he felt the fish stop moving, but the line was still heavy. Then the weight increased, and he let out more line. He felt the fishing line go straight down.

"The fish took it," he said. "Now I will let the fish enjoy his meal."

He let the line slip through his fingers. He prepared extra fishing lines with his left hand. Now he was ready. He had three 72-meters of extra line.

"Eat it a little more," he said. "Enjoy it."

"Eat it so that the point of the hook goes into your heart and kills you," he thought. "Come up and let me put the harpoon inside you. Well then. Are you ready? Have you eaten enough?"

"Now!" he said aloud.

He pulled up the fishing line with both hands. He had one extra meter of line. Then he pulled up the line again and again with all the strength in his arms.

Nothing happened. The fish just moved slowly away and the old man could not bring it up at all. His fishing line was strong; it was for heavy fish. He held the line and leaned back. The line was so tight. Then the line made a hissing sound in the water. The boat began to move slowly. It sailed northwest.

The fish moved ahead. The boat moved slowly on the calm water. The other baits were still in the water. The old man could not do anything.

"I wish the boy was here with me," the old man said out loud. "A fish is pulling my boat. I could tie the line to the boat. But the fish could break the line. I have to hold on. Thank God, the fish is not going down."

"What will I do if the fish goes down? I don't know. What if the fish goes down to the ocean floor and dies? I don't know. But I'll do something."

He held the line against his back and watched it. The boat was moving steadily to the northwest.

"If the fish keeps pulling the boat, it will die. The fish can't do this forever," the old man thought.

But the fish kept swimming and pulling the boat. Four hours passed. The old man still held the line against his back.

"It was noon when I hooked the fish," the old man said.

"I have never seen it."

Before he hooked the fish, he pushed his hat down on his head. It was too tight. His hat hurt his forehead. He was thirsty too. He got down on his knees and reached out carefully for his water bottle. He opened the water bottle and drank a little. He rested against the boat. He tried not to think of anything.

Then he looked behind him. There was no land in sight.

"That's not a problem. I can always go back," he thought. "The sun will set in two hours. Maybe the fish will come up before dark. If it doesn't, it will come up with the moon. My hands are fine and I feel strong. The fish has the hook in its mouth. The hook is hurting the fish. What a strong fish! It can pull a boat like this. I wish I could see it."

Chapter 10
Moving Along

The fish did not change its direction. The old man looked at the sky. There were stars. He knew the direction of the fish because he looked at the stars. After sunset, it was cold. The old man's sweat dried up. There was a sack. The old man dried the sack during the day. He tied the sack around his neck. The sack hung down over his back. The sack became the cushion for the old man and the fishing line. He was feeling a little better now. He was even a little comfortable.

"I can do nothing with the fish. The fish can do nothing with me," he thought.

He stood up and looked at the stars. He checked his course and the fishing line. The line was like a beam of light. The boat was moving more slowly. The light of Havana was not strong. He knew that the current was pushing the boat toward the east.

"If I can't see the light from Havana, then the boat is going toward the east," he thought.

"I wonder how today's baseball game went," he thought. "It would be nice to go fishing with a radio." Then he thought, "Focus on what you're doing."

Then he said out loud, "I wish I had the boy here. I wish he could help me. I wish he could see this."

"Old people should not be alone," he thought. "I must remember to eat the tuna tomorrow. I need to keep strong," he said to himself.

Two porpoises followed the boat during the night. He could hear the noise of porpoises. He could tell the difference between the sounds of the male and female porpoises.

"They are good," he said. "They are playful and they like games. They are our brothers like the flying fish."

Then he began to think of the fish. He felt sorry for the big fish.

"This fish is wonderful and strange. How old is this fish?" he thought. "I have never had such a strong fish. The fish isn't jumping around. It must be smart. Maybe the fish has been hooked a lot. It knows how to fight."

"The fish does not know that I'm an old man. But what a great fish! I can get a good price for the fish meat at the market. The fish bit the bait like a male. The fish has no fear," he thought.

He remembered the time he had caught one of a pair of marlin fish. The male fish always gives food to the female fish first. So the old man hooked a female marlin. The female marlin got scared. She fought a wild fight. She became tired after that. But the male fish stayed with the female fish. The male fish's tail was very sharp. The old man was afraid that the male fish would cut the line with his tail.

The old man grabbed the female fish. When the old man hit the female fish, the male fish stayed with the female fish. The male fish saw them bring the female fish onto the boat. The old man was clearing the lines and preparing the harpoon. The male fish jumped and went away.

"The male fish was beautiful," the old man remembered. "He stayed with the female."

"That was the saddest thing I ever saw with those fish," the old man thought.

"I wish the boy were here," he said out loud.

He leaned against the front of the boat. He felt the strength of the fish through the fishing line. The boat was still moving forward. The old man did not know where they were going.

"You, the fish, are the one who's been caught by me. Make your choice," the old man thought. "Your choice was to stay in the deep water. My choice was to go there to find you. Now we are joined together. There is no one to help either one of us. I was born to be a fisherman. I must remember to eat the tuna in the morning."

Chapter 11
Tug-of-war

Before it was light outside, something took one of the baits. The old man heard the stick break. And he heard the movement of the fishing line. The old man took out his knife in the darkness. Then he held the line with his shoulder. He held all the pressure of the weight of the fish. He cut that fishing line and also the line closest to him. He tied the cut lines together. He used one hand and one foot to work. Now he had six extra fishing lines, all tied together.

"After sunrise, I will cut the rest of the line and connect the extra spools," he thought. "I lost 360 meters of good fishing line and the hooks. That can be replaced. But who can replace this big fish? What was that other fish just now? I don't know. It could have been a marlin or a shark. I never felt the fish."

"I wish I had the boy," he said out loud.

"But you don't have the boy here," he thought. "You are by yourself. You need to work on the fishing line now."

He went to the back of the boat and cut the fishing lines. He tied the fishing lines. It was difficult to do this in the dark. Suddenly, the big fish moved and pulled him down on his face. There was blood below his eyes. He went to the front of the boat and he rested.

He adjusted the sack. He carefully shifted the fishing line

to a new part of his shoulders. He held the fishing line tightly. He felt the fish pulling on the line. He put his hand into the water. He felt the speed of the boat.

"I wonder what made the fish move suddenly," he thought. "The wire must have hurt the fish's back. My back must hurt more than its back. The fish cannot pull this boat forever. Now there is no problem."

"Fish," he said softly. "I'll stay with you until I die."

"The fish will stay with me too," the old man thought.

He waited for the morning light. It was cold because it was before daylight. He pushed against the wood to be warm.

"I can do it as long as the fish can," he thought.

The first light of the dawn came. The boat kept moving. When the sun came up, the fishing line was on the old man's right shoulder.

"He's headed north," the old man said.

"The current is moving us to the East," he thought. "I wish the fish would go with the current. The fish would get tired that way."

When the sun came up, the old man knew that the fish was not tired. There was only one good sign. The direction of the fishing line changed. That meant the fish was swimming upwards.

"God, let it jump," the old man said. "I have enough line to catch it."

"If I pull the fishing line, the fish will jump up." he thought.

He tried to tighten the fishing line. But the fishing line was already too tight. He felt the stiff line as he leaned back to pull it.

"I should not pull it," he thought. "If I pull it, the hook will come loose. When the fish jumps, it might throw the hook. Anyway, I feel better now. I do not have to look into the sun."

There was yellow weed on the fishing line. It became a heavier burden the fish dragged around. The yellow weed made a glowing light in the night.

"Fish," he said.

"I love you and respect you. But I will kill you before this day," he thought.

Chapter 12
A Small Bird

A small bird came toward the boat from the north. The bird was a warbler. The old man could see that the bird was very tired. The bird sat in the front of the boat and rested there. Then the bird flew around the old man's head. The bird rested on the fishing line.

"How old are you?" the old man asked the bird. "Is this your first trip?"

When he spoke, the bird looked at him. The bird was so tired. The bird did not look down at the line. The bird's feet held on tight.

"The line is steady," the old man said to the bird. "Why are you so tired when there was no wind last night?"

"The hawks will hurt these little birds," he thought.

But he didn't say that to the bird. The bird could not understand him anyway.

"Take a good rest, small bird," he said. "Then go and take your chance."

Talking to the bird like this helped the old man because his back hurt so much.

"Stay at my house if you want to," he said. "I'm sorry I can't take you back now, because I am with a friend."

Just then, the fish moved quickly. The old man fell down onto the boat. He gave the fish extra line, so he did not fall into the water. When the line was pulled, the bird flew away.

He felt the line gently with his right hand. He saw that his hand was bleeding.

"Something hurt the fish," he said out loud.

He tugged on the fishing line. But then the line became tight.

"You're feeling it now," he said to the fish. "And so am I."

He looked around for the bird. He wanted the bird to be with him. The bird was gone.

"You did not stay long," he thought. "It will be difficult to get to the land."

"How did I fall down with that one pull?" he thought. "I must be losing my mind. Or maybe I was thinking about the small bird. Now I will think about my work. I need to eat the tuna. I wish the boy were here. I wish I had some salt," he said out loud.

Chapter 13
Left Hand

The old man shifted the line to his left shoulder. He got down on his knees. He washed his hand in the ocean. He kept his hand in the water. The blood washed away. He watched the movement of the water against his hand.

"The fish really slowed down," he said.

The old man wanted to keep his hand in the saltwater. He was afraid that the fish might move. He stood up and held his hand up to the sunlight. The cut on his hand was not deep. It was only a burn from the line. But it was in an important part of his hand. The old man was upset because more work would start soon and he needed his hand.

"I need to eat the small tuna now," he said when his hand was dry. "I can reach the fish with the gaff."

He found the tuna in the boat. He dragged the tuna to him with the gaff. He held the fishing line with his left shoulder again. He also used his left hand and arm. He took the tuna off the gaff. He put a knee on the tuna. He cut the tuna from the back of the head to the tail. He cut the tuna into six pieces. He put them in front of the boat. He cleaned off his knife on his pants. He threw the rest of the tuna into the sea.

"I don't think I can eat all of this piece of fish," he said.

He moved his knife across the piece. The fishing line was

still tight. His left hand was cramped. He looked at his hand and felt sick.

"What is happening to my hand," he said. "Why do you have a cramp, hand? Fine. Make yourself into a claw. This will not be good for you."

He looked down into the water at the fishing line.

"Eat the tuna now, and it will make your hand strong," he thought. "My hand did not cause this. My hand has been working for many hours with the fish."

He picked up a piece of fish and put it in his mouth. He chewed it slowly. It tasted good.

"This would be good to eat with some lemon or salt," he thought.

"How do you feel, hand?" he asked his cramped hand that was very stiff.

"I'll eat some more for you."

He ate the other part of the piece of fish. He chewed it gently.

"How are you, hand? Is it too early to ask you?"

He ate another piece.

"The tuna is a strong and hearty fish," he thought. "I am happy to have a tuna instead of a dolphin. Dolphin meat is too sweet, but the tuna is not sweet."

But in that moment, he could not be fancy. He had to be practical.

"I have no salt. The fish might dry in the sun, or the fish

might go bad. I don't know what will happen. I am not hungry, but I have to eat all of this tuna. I will eat all of the tuna. I will be ready," he thought.

"Be patient, hand," he said. "I am doing this for you."
"I wish I could feed the fish," he thought. "The fish is my brother. But I must kill the fish."
He slowly ate all of the pieces of fish. He stood up straight and wiped his hand on his pants.

"Hand, you can let the fishing line go," he said. "I will hold the line with just my right arm."
He put his left foot on the heavy line. He rested against the strength of the line with his back.

"God, help my hand to recover," he said. "I don't know what the fish is going to do."
"The fish is peaceful," he thought. "What is the fish's plan? What is my plan? My plan will follow the fish's plan, because this fish is huge. If the fish jumps, I can kill it. If the fish stays down there forever, I will stay down with it forever."

He rubbed the cramped hand against his pants. He tried to warm up his fingers. But they would not open.
"Maybe my hand will open when the sun comes up high," he thought. "Maybe my hand will open when I digest the tuna. If I have to use my hand, I will open it. But I don't want to force it open. I should let it open slowly. I used this hand too much in the night."

Chapter 14
Jumping Up

He looked across the sea. He knew how alone he was now. But he could see rainbow shapes in the deep water. The clouds were coming together in the sky. He saw a group of wild ducks. The birds were spread out in the sky, then they gathered together. He knew no man was ever alone on the sea.

"Some men are afraid of being far from the land in a small boat," he thought. "Sometimes, there is bad weather out on the sea. It's the time of year for hurricanes. But if there are no hurricanes, the weather is nice."

If there is a hurricane coming, you can see changes in the sky. But it is hard to see these changes on land. The changes on land are different. But there is no hurricane now.

He looked at the sky. He saw wide clouds and thin clouds. The clouds looked like piles of ice cream.
"What a nice breeze," he said. "This is a great day for me."

His left hand was still cramped, it was opening little by little.
"I hate cramps," he thought. "My own body let me down. It's a shameful thing to have a stomach problem in front of people. But a cramp makes me feel ashamed of

myself."

"If the boy were here, he could rub my hand and my arm for me," he thought. "But it will be okay soon."

He felt the difference in the pull of the line with his right hand. He saw the fishing line move. He leaned against the line. He hit his left hand on his leg.

"The fish is coming up," he said. "Move, hand. Please move, hand."

The fishing line rose up slowly. The surface of the ocean splashed in front of the boat. The fish came out. He was bright, and his head and back were dark purple. The stripes on his sides were a light purple color. His sword was as long as a baseball bat. He came up from the water. Then he went back into the water peacefully. The old man saw the huge tail of the fish.

"The fish is 0.6 meters longer than the boat," the old man said.

The fishing line went down fast. The fish was not scared. The old man was trying to hold the fishing line with both hands. He knew that if he could not slow the fish down, the fishing line would break.

"He is a huge fish. I must catch him," he thought. "I must never let him know that he is very strong. If I were a fish, I would swim away with all my energy. But I am glad this fish is not smart like humans are."

The old man had seen many huge fish. He saw many fish that were more than 500 kilograms. He caught two of those fish in his life. But now he was trying to catch the biggest fish, alone. His left hand was still cramped.

"My hand will relax. The cramp will go away," he thought. "My left hand will relax to help my right hand. The fish and my two hands are brothers. I have to relax my hand."

The fish slowed down. It was going at the normal speed.

"I wonder why the fish jumped," the old man thought. "He showed me how big he was. Now, I know. I wish I could show him what kind of person I am. Let the fish think I am powerful. But the only thing I have to fight him is my will and my intelligence."

Chapter 15
The Prayer

The old man leaned against the boat. He was feeling comfortable. The fish swam along and the boat moved through the water. There was a small sea rising with wind coming up. The cramp in the old man's hand went away at noon.

"Bad news for you, fish," he said.

He moved the line over the sacks that covered his shoulders. He felt comfortable but he was still suffering.

"I'm not a man of faith," he said. "But I will pray the Lord's Prayer ten times so I can catch this fish. If I catch the fish, I will go to the Catholic Church. I promise."

He began to say the Lord's Prayer without thinking. Sometimes he would be so tired that he could not remember the prayer. But he kept praying.

After praying, he felt much better. He was still suffering. He leaned against the front of the boat. He began moving the fingers of his left hand mechanically. The breeze was rising softly but the sun was hot.

"I had better tie the bait to that little fishing line again," he said. "If the fish stays another night, I will need to eat again. I think I will catch a dolphin here. If I eat him fresh, he won't taste bad. I wish I could catch a flying fish. But I have no light to attract them. Flying fish are delicious. I don't even need to cut him up. I must save all my energy. I did not know this fish was so big. But I'll kill it."

"I will show him what a man can do and how he can survive," he thought.

"I told the boy that I was a strange old man," he said. "Now it's time to prove it."

He had proved it a thousand times. But that meant nothing. He was proving it again now. Each time was a new time.

"I wish the fish would fall asleep. I could sleep and dream about lions," he thought.

"Why do I dream of lions? Don't think, old man," he said to himself. "Take a rest in the boat, and don't think too hard."

The morning changed to afternoon. The boat still moved slowly and steadily. But there was a breeze from the east. It made the boat heavy. The fish slowed down. The weight of the fishing line on the old man's back became lighter.

Once in the afternoon, the fishing line came up again. But the fish only continued to swim a little bit. The sun was on the old man's left arm and his back. He knew the fish had turned to the east from the north.

He had seen the fish once. He could picture the fish swimming in the water with his fins stretched out like wings and his huge tail.

"I wonder how much the fish can see in the deep water," he thought.

"The fish has bigger eyes than a horse does. If a horse can see well in the dark, how well can this fish see in the dark?"

The sun and the movement of his fingers helped his left hand. His left hand recovered. He began to shift more weight onto the left hand. He shrugged the muscles of his back.

"If you are not tired, fish," he said out loud. "You must be very strange."

He felt very tired. He knew the night would come soon. He tried to think of other things. He thought of Major League Baseball. He knew there was a game between the New York Yankees and Detroit Tigers.

"This is the second day that I don't know the result of the games," he thought.

"But I must have confidence. I must be worthy of the great DiMaggio. He always does everything well, even with the bone pain in his heel. Is it as painful as having a pin in the foot? I don't think I could handle that. If I lost my eye, I could not endure. Humans are not as strong as some birds and other animals."

"I hope there are no sharks," he said out loud. "If sharks come up, there will be trouble."

"Would the great DiMaggio stay with this fish for a long time like I will stay with this one?" he thought. "I am sure he would. He is young and strong. His father was a fisherman. But would the bone pain hurt him too much?"

"I do not know," he said out loud. "I never had bone pain before."

Chapter 16
Arm Wrestling

As the sun set, he remembered the past. He wanted to give himself confidence. He remembered when he was in the bar. He played an arm wrestling game with a black man who was the strongest man.

They arm wrestled for one day and one night. Their elbows were on the table, and their forearms were straight. They gripped hands tight. Each one was trying to force the other's hand down. There was big money betting. People went in and out of the room under the lamplight. He looked at the black man's arm, hand and face.

There were referees there who controlled the game and made sure the rules were followed. The referees changed every four hours. Blood came out from their fingernails as they wrestled. They looked each other in the eye and at their hands and forearms. People went in and out of the room and sat on chairs near the wall and watched. The wooden walls were painted bright blue. The lamps made shadows on the walls. The black man's shadow was huge. The lamps kept moving with the breeze. Shadows moved as the lamps moved.

The winner would change back and forth all night. People gave some beer and cigarettes to the black man. The black man tried very hard. The old man, who was not an old man at that time, was nearly 8cm off balance. But the old man raised his hand up again. The old man was sure that he could win against the black man, who was a great athlete.

The morning came. The people wanted the game to be a draw. The referee also agreed. The old man suddenly tried his best and forced the black man's hand down. The black man's hand touched the table.

The game started on a Sunday morning and ended on a Monday morning. Many people asked for a draw. They had to go to work on the docks or at the Havana Coal Company. If they did not have work, everyone would have wanted the game to go on until it finished. But the old man won and finished the game on time.

For a long time after that, everyone had called him "The Champion." And there had been a return game in the spring. But people did not bet very much. He won the game again quite easily.

After that, he played a few games. Then he had stopped playing games. He could win against anyone if he wanted to. He decided that the games were bad for his right hand for fishing. He tried a few games with his left hand. But his left hand always disappointed him. He did not trust his left hand.

"The sun will warm my hands," he thought. "I don't want to get a cramp again. I have to stay warm tonight. I wonder what will happen tonight."

An airplane passed overhead. The plane was going to Miami. The old man watched the shadow of the airplane over the schools of flying fish.

"There are so many flying fish, there should be dolphins too," he said.

He tried pulling the fishing line to see his fish. But the fishing line didn't move at all. The boat moved along slowly. He watched the airplane until he could not see it.

"It must be very strange in an airplane," he thought. "I wonder what the sea looks like from up there? People in the airplane might be able to see the fish well. I would like to fly and see the fish from above."

"When I was on the turtle boat, I was on the mast. I could see many things from up there. The dolphin looks more green from there. You can see the dolphin's stripes and purple spots. You can see a whole school of dolphins. Why do all of the fast fish have purple backs, purple stripes, or purple spots? The dolphin looks green. But when it comes to feed, its stripes turn purple, like a marlin's stripes. What makes the stripes show up? Is it anger, or speed?"

Chapter 17
The Dolphin

It was just before dark. The boat passed a big island of yellow seaweed. The yellow seaweed moved up and down in the sea. It looked like the sea was playing with friends under a yellow blanket.

A dolphin took the old man's small line. He saw the dolphin when it jumped in the air. It looked golden in the sun. The dolphin was flapping in the air. The fish was afraid and it jumped again. The old man held the big fishing line with his right hand and arm.

When the fish came close by, he pulled the fish into the boat. The fish was jumping and moving from side to side. The fish moved its mouth quickly. The fish hit the boat with its long body. The old man clubbed the fish on its golden head.

The old man unhooked the fish. He re-baited the fishing line and tossed it into the sea. He moved slowly to the front of the boat. He washed his left hand and wiped it on his pants. Then he moved the fishing line from his right hand to his left hand. He washed his right hand in the sea while he watched the sun go down into the ocean.

"The fish hasn't changed at all," he said.
But, as he watched the movement of the water against his hand, he noticed that it was slower.
"I'll tie the two oars together across the boat. This will slow the fish down," he said. "Have a good night, fish."

"It would be better to eat a little later," he thought. "I'm going to tie the oars a little later too. It's better to leave the fish alone. Sunset is a difficult time for all fish."

He let his hand dry in the air. He grasped the fishing line with his right hand and relaxed as much as he could. He leaned forward against the boat. The boat took more of the pressure than he did.

"I'm learning now," he thought. "The fish hasn't eaten since it took the bait. And it is huge and needs a lot of food. I ate the whole tuna. And I will eat the dolphin tomorrow. I should eat some of the dolphin soon. It will be harder to eat than the tuna."

"How do you feel, fish?" he asked out loud. "I feel good and my left hand is better. I have food for one night and one day. Pull the boat, fish."

He did not truly feel good. The pain from the fishing line across his back had been there for so long. It felt very strange.

"But I have had worse things happen than that," he thought. "My hand has a little cut but the cramp is gone from my left hand. My legs are doing better. I have enough food too."

It was dark. The sun usually sets early in September. He lay in the front part of the boat and took a rest. The first star came out. He did not know the name of the star. This star was Rigel. He knew that stars would all come out soon. The stars were his friends.

"The fish is my friend, too," he said out loud. "I have never seen or heard of a fish like this. But I must kill this fish. I am glad people do not have to kill the stars."

"What if people had to kill the moon?" he thought. "The moon runs away from people."

Then he felt sorry for the great fish. The fish had nothing to eat. He still wanted to kill the fish.

"How many people deserve to eat this fish?" he thought. "Not many people are good enough to eat this amazing fish. Anyway, it is good that we do not have to try to kill the moon."

"I must think about tying the oars," he thought. "It has its risks and its benefits. If the fish pulls the boat with its tied oars, I may lose the fishing line and the fish. But if I don't tie the oars, this challenge will continue. This fish is able to go very fast. No matter what, I need to cut up the dolphin and eat it."

"I will rest for one hour more and then check on the fish. Then I will make the decision," he thought. "Meanwhile, I can see if he shows any changes. Trying the oars is a good idea. But safety is more important. The fish still has energy. I saw that the hook was in the corner of his mouth. The fish kept his mouth shut tight. The pain of the hook is nothing to this fish. Being hungry and fighting against strong forces will be difficult. Rest now old man, and let him work."

Chapter 18
Sleep

He thought he had rested for about two hours. The moon did not rise until late that night. He had no way to know what time it was. He didn't really rest. He was still pulling the fishing line across his shoulders. He placed his left hand on the boat. The pulling force of the fish shifted to the boat.

"It would be easy if I could tie the fishing line to something," he thought. "But with one small move, the fish could break the line. I have to support the fishing line with my body."

"But you haven't slept yet, old man," he said out loud. "You haven't slept for almost two days. The fish is calm now. You must think of a way that you can sleep. If you do not sleep, you might go crazy."

"My head is doing just fine. I am feeling bright like the stars."

"Still, I need to sleep. The stars, the moon, the sun, and even the ocean go to sleep. Don't forget to sleep," he thought. "I need to think of a way to take care of the fishing line."

"Now go back and prepare the dolphin. If you have to sleep, it is too dangerous to tie oars."

"I could go without sleeping," he told himself. "But it would be too dangerous."

He moved carefully to the back of the boat on his hands and knees. He thought he might be half asleep. But he did not want the fish to rest. "The fish must pull the boat until it dies."

In the back of the boat, the old man held the line tightly with his left hand.

He pulled out his knife with his right hand. The stars were bright. He saw the dolphin clearly. He pulled the dolphin up from the bottom of the boat with a knife. He put one of his feet on the fish and cut it in half from the tail to the mouth. Then he put the knife down. He cleaned out the inside of the fish with his right hand. He felt something inside the fish. There were two flying fish inside. They were fresh and hard. He dropped the other parts of the dolphin. The dolphin was cold. He skinned one side of the dolphin. Then he turned it over and skinned the other side.

He threw away the bones of the fish. He looked in the water. He watched it sink slowly. He put the flying fish into the two pieces of the dolphin. He put the knife back in its case. He went to the front of the boat. The fishing line was across his back. His back was bent. He carried the fish in his right hand.

He placed the two pieces of fish on the wood with the flying fish. He put the fishing line across his shoulders in a new place. He held the line again with his left hand. He leaned over the side of the boat and washed the flying fish in the water. He felt the speed of the water against his hand. His hand was dirty from skinning the fish. He watched the flow of the water touching his hand. He rubbed his hand against the boat. The flow of the water was less strong. The particles of fish on his hand went into the water.

"The fish is getting tired or the fish is resting," the old man said. "Let me eat all of this dolphin. Then I'll get some rest."

Under the stars with night getting colder, he ate half of one of the pieces and one of the flying fish.

"Dolphin is delicious when it's cooked, and terrible to eat when it's raw. I will never go in a boat again without salt," he said.

"I should have put sea water on the boat and when it dried, there would have been salt," he thought. "But I did catch the dolphin in the evening. I did not prepare for this. Now I am done eating."

The sky was getting cloudy in the east. The stars he knew were going away one by one. It looked like he was moving into a valley of clouds. The wind stopped.

"There will be bad weather," he said. "But not tonight and not tomorrow. Get some sleep, old man. The fish is calm now."

He held the fishing line in his right hand. He pushed his right hand with his thigh.

He leaned all his weight against the boat. He moved the

line a little lower and held it in his left hand.

"My right hand can hold the fishing line," he thought. "If my right hand relaxes in sleep, my left hand will wake me. This is difficult for the right hand. Even if I sleep for twenty minutes, it is good."

He lay forward on the fishing line with all of his body. He fell asleep.

Chapter 19
A Cut On the Hand

He did not dream of the lions. He dreamed of a school of porpoises. The school of porpoises was eight to ten miles wide. They would jump high into the air and return to the same spot. Then he dreamed that he was on his bed. There was a north wind. He was very cold. His head rested on his right arm instead of a pillow.

He began to dream of the yellow beach. He saw the first of the lions come to the beach. It was in the early evening. The other lions came. He rested his chin on the wood of the ship. He felt the breeze. He waited to see if more lions would come. He was happy. The moon had been up for a long time. He kept sleeping. The fish pulled the boat. The boat moved into the tunnel of clouds.

He woke up with his right fist punching his face. The fishing line slipped out through his right hand. He had no feeling in his left hand. He grabbed the line with his right hand, but the line rushed out. Finally, his left hand grabbed the line. He leaned back against the line. Then, the line burned his back and his left hand. His left hand took all the pressure.

He looked back at the spool of the fishing line. The line was moving. Just then, the fish jumped. It made a huge splash in the ocean, and then it fell down. The fish jumped again and again. The boat and the fishing line were moving fast. The old man held on to the fishing line. He had been pulled down onto the boat. His face was on the flesh of the dolphin. He could not move.

"This is what we waited for," he thought. "Let's take it. I will make the fish pay for the fishing line."

He could not see the fish jumping. He only heard the splashing in the ocean. The fishing line was cutting his hands. He knew this would happen. He tried to keep the line on the hard parts of his hand with scars. He tried to keep the line from cutting the palms of his hands and his fingers.

"If the boy were here with me, he would put water on the spools of line," he thought. "Yes. I wish the boy was here."

The fishing line kept going out. But it was going out slowly.

He got up and lifted his head. He pulled his face out of the slice of dolphin. He was on his knees and he stood up slowly. More fishing line was moving out slowly. He went back to the coils of line. He could not see the coils of line but his feet could feel them. There was a lot of line. The fish had to pull the line.

"The fish jumped more than a dozen times," he thought. The sack on the back of the fish is full of air now. The fish cannot go deep into the water to die. The fish will start swimming in a circle soon and then I must make him tired. I wonder what scared him so suddenly? Was the fish hungry? Maybe he felt fear. But he was such a strong fish. This is strange."

"Don't be afraid, old man," he said. "You're holding the line but you cannot get more line."

The old man held the line with his left hand and his shoulders. He washed his face after falling into the pieces of the dolphin. He was afraid that the smell of the dead dolphin would make him sick.

When his face was clean, he washed his right hand. Then he watched the first light come out before the sunrise.

"The fish is swimming to the east," he thought. "That means he is tired. He will have to swim in a circle soon."

He looked at his right hand.

"It is not bad," he said. "And pain does not matter to a man."

He held the fishing line carefully. He was careful not to let the line touch the new wounds in his hand. He put his left hand into the sea on the other side of the boat.

"You were badly hurt, but it was worth it," he said to his left hand.

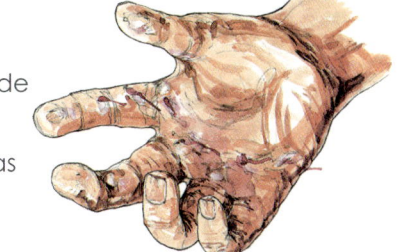

"Why don't I have two good hands?" he thought. "Maybe this is my problem. I didn't train my two hands well. But my left hand had many chances to learn. My left hand did a good job. The left hand only had one cramp. If my left hand has another cramp, I will let the line cut him off."

When he started to go crazy, he thought about chewing some more of the dolphin.

"But I can't," he told himself. "It is better to go crazy than to eat more dolphin. I will keep it for an emergency."

"You're a fool," he told himself. "Eat the other flying fish."

The flying fish was there. It was clean and ready to eat. He picked up the flying fish with his left hand. He ate it and chewed the bones.

"Flying fish is a healthy food," he thought. "This fish will give me strength. I have done what I can do. The fish will begin to swim in a circle. I'm ready."

Chapter 20
Circle

The sun was rising for the third time since he had gone out to sea to go fishing. He could not tell if the fish was swimming in a circle. The line was loose. He pulled the line gently with his right hand. The fishing line began to come in slowly.

He moved the line forward. He began to pull in the line gently. He used both of his hands in a swinging motion. He tried to pull with his body. His legs turned as he pulled the fishing line.

"It is a very big circle," he said. "But he is swimming in a circle."

Then the fishing line would not come in anymore. He held the line until he saw drops of water coming out of it. The fish started to pull the line. The old man knelt down. He let the line go back into the water.

"Now, the fish is making the outside part of his circle," he said.

"I must hold on to the line for a long time," he thought. "The fish will pull and his circle will get smaller. Maybe I will see the fish in one hour. I must kill him."

But the fish continued to swim in a circle. Two hours went by. The old man was wet with sweat. His bones were tired.

But the circles were smaller.

The old man saw black spots in front of him for one hour. The sweat made salt go into his eyes. The sweat made salt go into the cut on his forehead. He was not afraid of the black spots. He knew he would see black spots, since his body was stressed as he pulled the line. But he also felt dizzy and sick. He was worried.

"I can't die here with this fish right in front of me," he said. "The fish is coming up now. God, help me to keep going. I will pray the Lord's Prayer one hundred times."

The old man felt a strong pull on the line. It felt very heavy.

"The fish is hitting the wire on the fishing line with his spear," he thought. "I knew that he would do that. This may make him jump up. I hope he just swims in circles. If the fish jumps, he may escape from the hook."

"Don't jump, fish," he said. "Don't jump."

The fish hit the wire of the line again and again. The old man gave the fish a little more line each time.

"I must not pull too hard," he thought. "I can't give the fish more pain than this. My pain is okay. I can control my pain. But the fish is in so much pain that he might go crazy."

After a while, the fish stopped hitting the wire. The fish started swimming in a circle again. The old man was pulling in more line. He felt like he was going to faint again.

He lifted up some sea water. He put the sea water on his head. He also put sea water on his neck.

"I have no cramps," he said. "The fish will come up soon. I think I can stay alive."

He knelt against the boat. He slid the line over his back for a moment.

"I'll rest now while the fish swims in a circle," he thought. "I'll stand up when the fish comes close again."

The old man wanted to rest for about half an hour. But the fish turned around and came back to the boat. The old man stood up and pulled again.

"I'm more tired than ever," he thought. "The wind from the east is blowing. The wind will help me pull in the fish. I need this wind."

"I will take a rest when the fish swims out again," he said. "I feel better now."

His hat was on the back of his head. He sat down and felt the fish swim.

"You do the work, fish," he thought. "I'll meet you when you swim back to the boat."

The waves were getting higher. A calm breeze was blowing and the old man needed it to get home.

"I will go to the southwest," he said. "Cuba is a long island. I will find the shore."

Chapter 21
The Death of the Marlin

The old man saw the fish as it swam around the boat. The fish swam around the boat a third time. He was so surprised. The fish was very long.

"No, it can't be that big," he said.

But the fish really was that big. The fish came to the top of the water about thirty meters away from the boat. The old man saw the fish's tail come out of the water. The tail was bigger than a tall sword and it was a light purple color. The fish swam just below the top of the water. He could see the huge body of the fish. The fish had purple stripes on his body, and his fins were stretched out.

The old man could see the eye of the fish as it swam in a circle. Two gray sucker fish were also there. The sucker fish swam around the big fish. Sometimes they were connected to the fish. Sometimes they were away from the fish. Sometimes they swam in the fish's shadow. They were more than three feet long. When they swam fast, they moved like smooth, long fish.

The old man was sweating, but this was not from the sun. When the fish turned, the old man pulled in more line. He knew he would have a chance to put the fish with his harpoon.

"I must bring him close to me," he thought. "I must push the harpoon into his heart."

"Be calm and strong, old man," he said.

The next time the fish turned around, his back was out of the water. The fish was higher out of the water when he turned around again, but he was still too far away. The old man knew that the fish would come closer soon. His harpoon was ready. It had been ready for a long time. The harpoon was tied tightly to a rope and also tied to the boat.

The fish continued to swim in a circle. It was calm and beautiful. The fish moved his great tail. The old man pulled on the line to bring the fish closer. For a moment the fish turned a little on his side.

"I turned the fish," the old man said. "I turned the fish."

The old man felt dizzy again. He held on to the line as tightly as he could.

"I made him turn over," he thought. "Maybe this time I can pull him over the side of the boat."

"Come on, hands! Pull!" he thought. "Hold on, legs! Keep going, head! You never gave up!"

But when the old man pulled with all his strength, the fish turned and swam away.

"Fish, you will have to die sometime," the old man said. "Do you have to kill me too?"

"That will not do anything," he thought.

His mouth was too dry to speak. He could not reach the water.

"I must make him swim next to the boat," he thought.

"I don't have much strength left. No, you have strength," he told himself. "You still have strength."

The old man almost caught the fish when he swam by again, but the fish swam away once more.

"You are killing me," the old man thought. "But you have a right to do that. I have never seen a greater or more beautiful fish than you, fish. Come on and kill me. I do not care who kills who."

"I'm getting confused," he thought. "Clear your head. Think about how to keep going."

"Clear up, head!" he said in a little voice. "Clear up."

The fish swam in a circle two more times. The same thing happened.

"I do not know what to do now," the old man thought. "But I will try again."

He tried once more, and he felt dizzy when he tried to catch the fish. Nothing changed. The fish swam away.

"I will try again," the old man promised.

The old man's hands and eyes were tired. He tried again and it was the same.

"I will try again," he thought.

The old man used his pain, his strength, and his pride to

fight the fish. The fish came close to the boat. He swam gently on his side and his nose almost touched the boat. Then he started to pass by the boat.

The old man dropped the fishing line. He put his foot on the line. He lifted the harpoon and shoved it down with all his strength. The harpoon went into the fish's chest. The old man shoved it deep into the fish.

The fish jumped up one more time. The fish showed his length and all his power. The fish stayed in the air for a while. Then it fell into the water. There was a splash in the ocean and water went into the boat.

The old man felt dizzy and sick. He could not see well. He cleared the harpoon line. He let the harpoon line move slowly through his hands. The fish had turned over with his silver belly up. The harpoon was deep in the fish. The sea was full of blood from the heart of the fish. The blood looked like a school of fish. Then the blood spread out like a cloud. The fish was a silver color and it floated on the waves.

Chapter 22
Tying the Marlin to the Boat

The old man looked for a moment. He tied the harpoon line around the front of the boat. He placed his head in his hands.

"I must be strong," he said. He leaned on the boat. "I am a tired old man. But I killed this fish. Now I have to work."

"I must prepare the rope to tie him to the side of the boat," he thought. "If I put the fish in the boat, the boat will sink. I need to prepare everything. I will bring the fish closer and tie him up. I will put up the mast and sail back home."

He started to pull the fish up to the side of the boat.

"I want to see him," he thought. "I want to touch and to feel him. He is my prize."

"When I pushed the harpoon into him, I think I felt his heart. I will bring in the fish and tie him to the boat."

"Get to work, old man," he said.

He drank a little water.

"There's so much work to be done."

He looked at the sky. He looked at the sun carefully.

"Maybe it's noon," he thought. "The wind from the east is blowing. I can fix the fishing line when I go home."

"Come on, fish," he said.

But the fish did not come. The old man pulled the boat

up to the fish.

When he was close to the fish, he looked at the fish's head. He could not believe how large the fish was. He untied the harpoon rope. He pushed the rope through the fish's gills and out through his mouth. He tied the fish's head to the boat with the rope. He tied the fish's tail to the back of the boat. The fish's color changed from purple to silver, but the stripes were the same color. The stripes were wider than a man's hand. The fish's eye looked empty.

"That was the only way to kill him," the old man said. He felt better after he drank some water. His head was clear.

"The fish is over 1,500 pounds," he thought. "If the head, tail, and fins are cut off, the fish will be 1,000 pounds. How much will it cost if it is 30 cents a pound?"

"I need a pencil for that," he said. "My head is not that clear. But I think the great DiMaggio would be proud of me. I have no bone pain. But my hands and my back hurt."

He tied the fish to the front and back of the boat. The fish was bigger than the boat. He cut a piece of line and tied the fish's mouth closed. He raised the mast and set up the sail of the boat. The boat began to move. He rested in the boat and sailed southwest.

He did not need a compass to show him where southwest was. He just needed to feel the wind.

"I need to put out a small fishing line," he thought. "I need to get something to eat and drink."

But he could not find any bait. So he hooked a yellow Gulf weed with the gaff. He shook the yellow Gulf weed and some small shrimps fell onto the boat. There were more than a dozen shrimps. The old man pulled off their heads with his finger. He ate all of them. He chewed up the shells and tails of the shrimps. The shrimps were small, but they were a healthy meal. They also tasted good.

The old man still had two sips of water left. He drank half of one sip after eating the shrimps. The boat was sailing well. He could see the fish. He could look at his hurting hands and feel the pain in his back. He knew that this was true. It was not a dream. When he fought the fish, he thought that maybe it was a dream. When the fish came out of the water and hung in the sky, he thought that he was dreaming again.

He could not believe it. But now he saw everything.

Now he knew the fish was real. The pain in his hands was not a dream.

"My hands will recover quickly," he thought. "My hands are not bloody anymore and the salt water will heal them. Salt water is the best medicine for my hands. All I have to do is keep the head clear. The hands have done their work."

Then his head started to become unclear.

He thought to himself. "Is the fish pulling me in or am I pulling the fish in? I'm not pulling the fish behind the boat and the fish is not in the boat with me. What's happening?"

"Well, the fish can pull me in if he wants to. He didn't hurt me."

Chapter 23
The Mako Shark

They sailed well, and the old man dipped his hands in the salt water. Clouds were high in the sky. The old man kept checking on the fish. It was an hour before the first shark came up to him.

The shark was not a surprise. The shark came up from the deep down in the water. He smelled the cloud of blood. The blood spread out in the deep sea. The shark jumped up from the water. Then he fell into the sea and smelled the blood again. The shark followed the boat.

Sometimes he could not find the smell of the fish, but then he would catch the smell again. The shark swam fast and followed the boat. He was a very big Mako shark. This shark could swim as fast as the fastest fish in the sea. Everything about this shark was beautiful, except for his mouth. His back was blue like the back of a swordfish. His belly was silver. The Mako shark looked like a swordfish, but his mouth was different. It swam under the surface of the water. Inside his mouth, he had eight rows of teeth. His teeth pointed inwards. They were shaped like claws. The shark's teeth were as long as human fingers. Sharks are made to eat all the fish in the sea. They are so fast and strong. Sharks will always win. Now the shark sped up. His blue fin zipped through the water.

When the old man saw the shark coming, he knew that the shark was not afraid. He prepared the harpoon. He tied the rope to the harpoon. He watched the shark come up to the boat. His head was clear. He was ready to fight, but he did not have hope. He looked at the huge fish. He watched the shark swim close.

"I wish this was a dream," he thought. "I can't stop the shark from getting to the fish. But maybe I can kill the shark."

The shark came close to the boat. When the shark came up to the fish, the old man saw his mouth open. The old man saw the shark's strange eyes, his teeth moving up and down. The shark's head was out of the water and his back was coming out too. The old man could hear the noise of the shark eating the fish. He drove the harpoon into the middle of the shark's head, where the shark's brain was. The old man drove the harpoon into the brain with all his strength.

The shark turned over. The old man saw that the shark's eyes had no life in them. The shark turned over again. The old man knew that the shark was dead. But the shark was still fighting. The shark's tail splashed in the water. His mouth moved and clicked. The water was white where his tail hit it. His body was above the water. The shark lay there for a little. Then he went down into the water very slowly.

"The shark took about forty pounds of meat from the

fish," he said out loud.

"He took my harpoon and all the rope," he thought. "My fish is bleeding again and other sharks will come."

He did not like to look at the fish anymore. When the shark bit the fish, the old man felt upset.

"But I killed the shark that bit my fish," he thought. "He was the biggest Mako shark that I have ever seen."

"That was a good moment, but it will change soon," he thought. "I wish it was a dream. I wish that I never caught this fish. I wish I was alone in bed."

"But a man cannot lose," he said. "A man can be crushed, but he cannot lose."

"I wish I hadn't killed the fish," he thought. "Now the bad time is coming and I do not even have the harpoon. The Mako sharks are cruel, strong, and smart. But I was smarter than the shark was."

"Maybe not," he thought. "Maybe it was because I had the harpoon."

"Don't think, old man," he said out loud. "Keep sailing this way."

"But I must think," he thought. "Because thinking is all I have left—thinking and baseball. I hit the shark in the brain. I wonder what the great DiMaggio would think? Were my hands hurting as much as his bone pain? I don't know. I have never had a problem with my heel."

"Think about something joyful, old man," he said. "You

are getting closer to home every minute. The boat became forty pounds lighter."

He knew what would happen when the boat went through the waves. But there was nothing he could do.

"Yes there is," he said out loud. "I can tie my knife to an oar. I may be an old man, but I am armed."

The breeze was fresh now and he continued to sail. He only checked on the front part of the fish. The old man became hopeful.

"It is silly to have no hope," he thought. "If I have no hope, it's a sin."

"Do not think about sin," he thought. "You have enough problems now. I don't understand sin. Maybe it was a sin to kill the fish. Do not think about sin. You were born to be a fisherman and the fish was born to be a fish."

But he liked to think about everything that he did. There was nothing to read and he did not have a radio. So he kept on thinking about sin.

"You didn't kill the fish to sell it for food," he thought. "You killed the fish because you have pride and because you are a fisherman. You loved the fish. If you love the fish, it is not a sin to kill him."

"You think too much, old man," he said out loud.

"But you enjoyed killing the Mako shark," he thought.

He eats fish to stay alive. He is beautiful and he is not afraid.

"I killed him to protect myself," the old man said out loud. "I killed him well."

"Everything kills something in some way," he thought. "Fishing kills me and fishing keeps me alive. Well, the boy keeps me alive."

He leaned against the boat. He pulled out a piece of the meat from the fish where the shark had taken a bite. He chewed it and tasted it. It was delicious. It was firm and juicy. He knew that it would bring a very high price at the market. But the old man knew that a very hard time was coming.

Chapter 24
The Two Sharks

The breeze was blowing. The wind changed. It did not slow down. The old man looked ahead of him. He could not see any smoke or any other boats. He only saw flying fish and yellow seaweed.

He sailed for two hours. He sometimes chewed on some meat from the marlin. He tried to rest and be strong. He saw the first of two sharks. "Ay!" he said out loud.

There is no way to say this word in English. Maybe it was like the noise someone makes if a hammer hits their finger.

"Shark," he said out loud.

He saw the second shark coming up behind the first. These were shovel-nosed sharks. He saw their brown fins and the movements of their tails. They smelled the blood of the fish. The sharks were very excited. They were coming closer to the boat.

He picked up the oar with the knife tied to it. He held the oar tightly. He watched the sharks coming. He could see their wide, shovel-pointed heads and their wide fins. The sharks hated everything. They smelled bad.

They were killers and they ate everything. They could eat the oars of a boat, the legs of turtles, or even humans. If they were hungry, they would eat a person, even if the person did not smell like blood.

"Ay," the old man said. "Sharks. Come on sharks."

They came. But they did not come up like the Mako sharks. One shark went under the boat. The shark pulled on the fish and bit it. The old man felt the boat shake. The other shark watched the old man. Then the shark came up to the fish and chewed on it. The old man could see the shark's head. The old man drove the knife into the shark's eyes. The shark let go of the fish and sank into the water.

The boat was still shaking. The other shark was eating the fish. The old man made the boat swing around. The shark came out from under the boat. When he saw the shark, he poked the shark with his knife. The knife didn't go very deep. This hurt the old man's hands and his shoulder. Then the shark came up again. He poked the middle of the shark's head. Then he poked the same spot again. The shark held on to the fish with his mouth.

The old man hit him in his left eye. But the shark still held on.

"No?" the old man said and he hit the shark's head again.

He felt a bone break. The old man put the oar into the shark's mouth to open it. The shark slid down into the water.

"Go on shark. Slide down deep. Go see your friend," he said.

The old man wiped his knife and put down the oar. He

brought the boat onto its course.

Chapter 25
The Broken Knife

"The sharks have taken a quarter of the fish," he said out loud. "I wish it were a dream and that I had never caught this fish."

He stopped to say this. He did not want to look at the fish. The fish had no blood left. It was now a silver color.

"I shouldn't have gone out so far," he said. "I'm sorry, fish."

"Now," he said to himself. "You need to make sure the knife is tied up. Rest your hands for now. Sharks will come again."

"I wish I had a stone for the knife," the old man said.

"I should have brought a stone."

"You needed to bring so many things," he thought. "But you did not bring them, old man. Now is not the time to think about what you do not have."

"You give me too much advice," he said out loud. "I'm tired of it."

The boat sailed along. The old man put his hands in the water.

"How much did that shark eat?" he said. "The boat is much lighter now."

He did not want to think about the part of the fish that the sharks ate. He knew that the sharks had chewed on the fish. The fish made a trail for the sharks to smell.

"Maybe this fish would keep me busy all winter," he thought. "Don't think of that. Just rest and try to prepare your hands well."

The blood smell from my hands does not matter. The blood smell from the fish is stronger. My hands are not bleeding now.

"What can I think of now?" he thought. "Nothing. I don't need to think. I will wait for the next ones to come."

"I wish it was a dream," he thought. "But who knows? Maybe the dream would end well."

The next shark to come was a shovel-nosed shark. He came up like a hungry pig with a big mouth. The old man let the shark bite the fish. Then the old man poked the shark in the brain with his knife. But the shark moved back. The knife broke.

The old man prepared to sail again. He didn't even watch the big shark sink down in the water. The shark went from a normal size, then a small size, and then a tiny size as it sank down.

"I have the gaff," he said. "But it will not be helpful. I have the two oars and the short club."

"Now the sharks will win," he thought. "I am too old to beat the sharks with a club. But I will try to do it."

He put his hands in the water again. It was getting late in

the afternoon. He saw only the sea and the sky. There was more wind now. He hoped to see land soon.

"You're tired," he said. "You're tired inside."

The sharks did not come again until the evening. The old man saw their brown fins coming. They headed straight for the boat swimming side by side.

He stopped the boat. He tied the sail line. He reached under the boat for the club. The club was made from an oar. He could only use the club with one hand. He held the club and watched the sharks come to the boat. There were two sharks.

"I will wait until the shark bites the fish," he thought. "Then I will hit him on the point of the nose or on top of the head."

The two sharks came close to the boat together. The shark that came close to him opened his mouth. The shark chewed on the fish. The old man raised his club up high. He pushed it down on top of the shark's head. He hit the shark once more across the nose.

The other shark went in and out. Then the other shark swam up again with his mouth open. The old man saw a piece of the fish in the shark's mouth. He swung at him and he could only hit the head. The shark looked at him and bit the fish one more time. The old man hit him with the club. The shark moved away.

"Come on, Shark," the old man said. "Come in again."

The shark swam up to him quickly. The old man hit him. He lifted the club up high and pushed it down. He felt the bone in the shark's head. He hit the shark again. The shark chewed on the meat. The shark moved away slowly.

The old man watched for the shark to come again. But the sharks did not come. Then he saw a shark swimming in circles. He did not see the fin of the other shark.

"I couldn't kill them," he thought. "But I did hurt them. Both of them must feel really bad right now. If I used two hands, I could have killed the first shark."

Chapter 26
Half of the Fish

He did not want to look at the fish. He knew that half of the fish had been eaten by sharks. While he was busy with the sharks, the sun went down.

"It will be dark soon," he said. "Soon I will see the lights of Havana."

"I can't be too far out," he thought. "I hope no one has been worried. The boy is the only one who is worried about me. Many older fishermen will worry too. I live in a good town."

He could not talk to the fish anymore. The sharks destroyed most of the fish. Then something came into his head.

"Half fish," he said. "I am sorry that I went too far out. But we killed many sharks. We wounded many others. How many sharks did you ever kill, old fish? You had to use that spear on your head for something."

"If the sharks and the big fish fought each other, who would win?" he thought. "The big fish has a spear on his nose. The spear is a good weapon. I wish I had cut off the fish's spear and fought the sharks."

"What will you do if the sharks come in the night? What can you do?" he said to himself.

"Fight them," he said. "I will fight them until I die."

It was already night. There was no light. There was only the wind and the sail. He felt like he was already dead. He put his two hands together. He felt pain.

He leaned against the boat. He was not dead. His pain told him. He was alive.

"I promised if I caught the fish I would pray," he thought. "But I am too tired to pray now."

He lay in the boat and looked for the light to come.

"I have half of the fish," he thought. "I wish I could bring some of the fish home. I think I have some luck."

"No," he said. "You ran out of luck when you went too far out."

"Don't be silly," he said out loud. "You may have some luck in the end."

"I'd like to buy some luck if there's a place where they sell it," he said.

"What could I buy luck with?" he asked himself. "Could I buy it with a lost harpoon, broken knife, and hurting hands?"

"You might be able to," he said. "You tried to buy luck with eighty-four days at sea."

"I must not think nonsense," he thought. "How could you buy it when you can't see luck? But I want to buy some luck somehow."

"I wish I could see the light," he thought.

He tried to sit comfortably. He felt pain. He knew he was still alive.

Chapter 27
The Last Fight

He saw the city lights in the distance. It was about ten o'clock at night. The lights were only a dim light in the sky. He could see the lights from across the ocean. He sailed on toward the lights.

"Now it is over," he thought. "The sharks will probably come again. How can I fight them without any weapons in the dark?"

He was stiff and in pain. His whole body was in pain. The night was very cold.

"I hope I don't have to fight again," he thought. "I really hope I don't have to fight again."

But he fought more sharks at midnight. He could not fight well. The sharks came in a group. He could see the lines of the shark fins. He hit the sharks with his club. The sharks shook the boat. He could not see the sharks, but he could feel them and hear them. Something grabbed his club and swam away.

He pulled out the lever. He held it in both hands. He fought the sharks with the lever. He pushed it down on them again and again. The sharks came together. They bit pieces of the fish. They came back for more.

Finally, one more shark came to the fish. The old man knew that the fight was now over. He swung the lever and hit the shark. He swung the lever again and again. The lever broke. The broken part was sharp. The old man pushed the

lever into the shark. The shark swam away. That was the last shark. There was nothing else for the sharks to eat.

The old man could hardly breathe. He tasted something in his mouth. It was blood. The old man spat it out.

"Eat that, sharks," he said. "You wish you could kill a man."

He knew the sharks had beaten him. He went to the back of the boat. He found part of the lever. He put the lever in its place. He sailed the boat again.

The boat became lighter. The old man didn't have any thoughts or any feelings. The old man sailed the boat to make it to his home port. The sharks bit the bones of the fish in the night. The old man did not focus on the sharks. He only focused on sailing.

"The boat is good," he thought. "The boat is safe and not harmed. Only the lever broke."

He could see the lights of the beach. He knew where he was now.

"Anyway the wind is our friend," he thought. "Sometimes the wind is our friend. Sometimes the sea is our friend too. The sea has friends and enemies underneath."

"And my bed is my friend. Going to bed will be so good," he thought. "Bed is a good friend when you are tired."

"What beat you?" he thought.

"Nothing," he said out loud. "I went out too far."

When he sailed into the little harbor, the Terrace's lights were out. He knew everyone was in bed. The breeze was stronger now. It was quiet in the harbor. He sailed onto some small rocks. There was no one to help him. He pulled the boat up as far as he could. Then he stepped out. He tied the boat to a rock.

He pulled the mast. He folded the sail and tied it. He carried the mast on his shoulder. He started to climb. He was so tired. He stopped for a moment. He looked back and saw the fish. He could only see the white line of the fish's bones.

He started to climb again. He fell when he came to the top. He stayed there for a while with the mast on his shoulder. He tried to get up. It was too difficult. He sat there with the mast on his shoulder. He looked at the road. A cat passed by. The old man watched the cat. Then he just watched the road.

Finally, he put the mast down and stood up. He picked up the mast and put it on his shoulder. He walked up the road. He had to sit down five times before he came to his cottage.

He leaned the mast on the wall. He found a water bottle and took a drink.

He lay down on the bed. He pulled the blanket over his body. He slept with his face down on the newspapers.

Chapter 28
At Home

The old man was sleeping when the boy came through the door. The boy came to the old man's cottage every day to check on him. But today he had slept late. He saw the old man sleeping there. The old man was breathing. The boy started to cry. He went out to buy some coffee for the old man. The boy kept crying as he walked along the road.

Many fishermen were looking at the old man's boat. Only the fish's bones were left. One of the fishermen was measuring the length of the bones. The boy did not go down. He had been there earlier.

"How is he?" one of the fishermen shouted.

"Sleeping," the boy called.

The boy was still crying.

"Let him sleep more."

"This fish was 5.5 meters from nose to tail," the fisherman said.

"I believe it," the boy said.

The boy went into the Terrace. He asked for a can of

coffee.

"Make the coffee hot and add a lot of milk and sugar, please."

"Do you want anything else?" the owner asked.

"No. After this I will see what he can eat."

"Do you want a drink?"

"No," the boy said. "Tell them not to bother Santiago. I'll be back."

"Tell Santiago how sorry I am." the owner said.

"Thanks," the boy said.

The boy carried the coffee up to the old man's cottage. The boy sat by the old man until he woke up. The old man started to wake up, but he fell asleep again. The boy waited for a long time. Finally, the old man woke up.

"Don't sit up," the boy said. "Drink this."

The old man took the coffee and drank it.

"I lost, Manolin," he said. "I lost the fight."

"No, you did not lose. You got the fish."

"I lost after I caught the fish."

"Pedrico is looking after the boat. What about the fish's head?"

"Let Pedrico keep the head."

"And the spear?"

"If you want it, you can keep it."

"I want it," the boy said.

"Now we must make plans about other things."

"Did they search for me?"

"Of course. They searched for you with the coast guard and with planes."

"The ocean is very big and the boat is small," the old man said.

He was happy to talk to someone instead of talking to himself.

"I missed you," he said. "What did you catch?"

"I caught one on the first day, one on the second day, and two on the third day," the boy said.

"Very good."

"Now we will fish together again."

"No. I am not lucky. I am not lucky anymore."

"I will bring the luck with me," the boy said.

"I caught two fish yesterday. But I have so much to learn from you. Let's fish together."

"We must get a good killing spear. We need a strong spear. My knife broke."

"I'll get another knife for us," the boy said. "I'll prepare a strong spear. What about the wind? Will we have any windy days soon?"

"We might have three windy days. Maybe more."

"I will have everything ready," the boy said. "Take care of your hands, old man."

"I know how to care for my hands. There was blood in my mouth last night. I think I broke something."

"Take care of that too," the boy said.

"Lie down, old man. I will bring you your clean shirt. I will bring you something to eat."

"Bring me the newspapers from when I was gone," the old man said.

"You must take a good rest. Did you have a hard time?"

"It was a very hard time," the old man said.

"I'll bring the food and the newspapers," the boy said. "Rest well, old man. I will bring something from the pharmacy. I will bring something to help your hands."

"Don't forget to tell Pedrico that he can keep the fish's head."

"I will tell him."

As the boy went out the door he was crying again. That afternoon, there were tourists at the Terrace. They were having a party. A woman saw the fish's long, white backbone with its huge tail.

"What's that?" she asked a waiter.

"It's a shark," the waiter said.

"I didn't know that sharks had such beautiful tails."

Up the road, in the old man's cottage, he was sleeping again. He was still sleeping face down. The boy was sitting beside him watching him. The old man was dreaming about the lions.